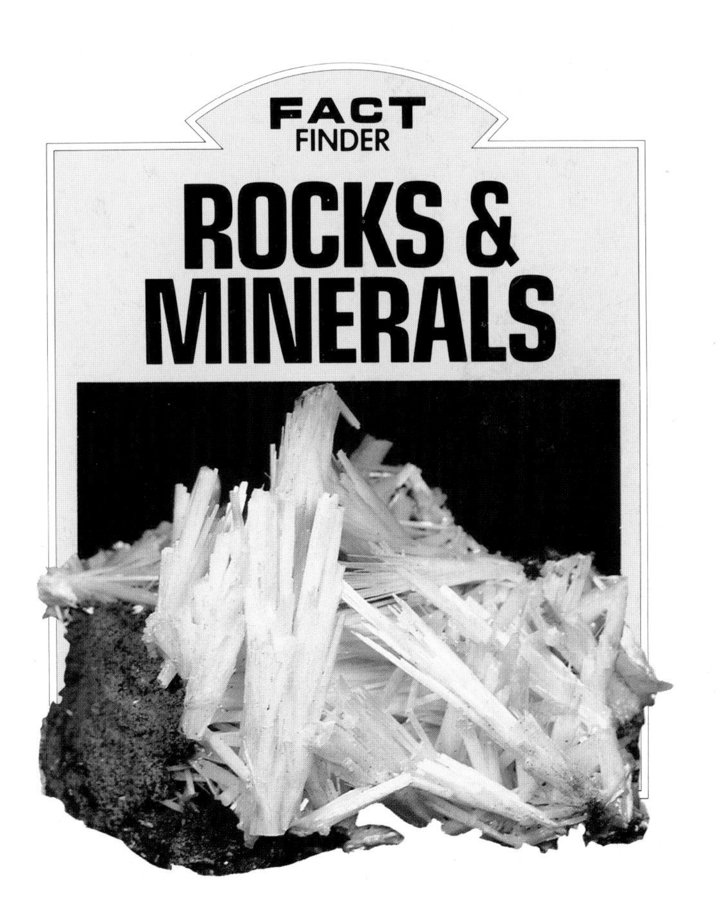
FACT
FINDER
ROCKS &
MINERALS

ROCKS & MINERALS

CHRIS · PELLANT

CRESCENT BOOKS
New York

A Salamander Book

First published by Salamander Books Ltd,
129–137 York Way,
London N7 9LG,
United Kingdom.

This 1990 edition published by Crescent Books,
distributed by Outlet Book Company Inc., a Random
House company, 225 Park Avenue South,
New York, New York 10003.

Credits

Editors: Tony Hall, Mark Bathurst

Designer: Paul Johnson

Color artwork: © Salamander Books Ltd

Printed and bound in Belgium

ISBN 0-517-05148-6

87654321

Acknowledgements

I would not have been able to produce this book without the help of a number of people. Many of the specimens I have photographed are in the collection of Cleveland County Leisure Services, and the county geologist, Ken Sedman, has allowed me access to this fine material and has always been ready to give help and advice. Jim Nunney, at Leeds City Museum, has also provided specimens for photography. My wife, Helen, has given support and encouragement throughout the project and has read proofs with meticulous attention to detail. She has also helped with typing and has compiled the index. Emily, my daughter, has allowed the extensive use of her typewriter, without which the book could not have been written. My two sons, Daniel and Adam, have tried to keep quiet when required.

THE AUTHOR AND PHOTOGRAPHER

Chris Pellant has been professionally involved with the Earth Sciences since graduating from Keele University, Staffordshire, in the United Kingdom. He lectures in geology, ecology and photography in both further and higher education and has appeared on television and radio. His writing has appeared in many books and periodicals, and a great number of his photographs have been published world-wide. *Rocks and Minerals* is his third book. Chris Pellant is a committed conservationist, being a member of the conservation pressure group Greenpeace, and an active member of many national geological and natural history societies.

CONTENTS

INTRODUCTION

Rocks and minerals are the materials of which the Earth's crust is made. They are often of striking beauty and great economic significance. As a result of the processes of weathering and erosion acting on rocks, the amazing landforms of our planet's surface are created. Minerals have been collected and prized for thousands of years and certain minerals still form the basis of our economic system. A study of rocks and minerals is part of our search for an understanding of the origins, formation and evolution of the Earth. In this book rocks are considered first. The primary, igneous rocks are followed by the sedimentary and metamorphic rocks, both these latter kinds resulting from recycling of existing rock material. The second part of the book deals with minerals. In the space available only a few of the many rocks and minerals can be described and illustrated; those chosen are examples from the main groups, showing typical features and something of the great variety that exists.

IGNEOUS ROCKS

Rocks have been defined as aggregates of mineral particles. This definition covers a very wide range of materials, from solid granite, in which the grains are literally welded together, to incoherent desert sand. Generally, however, when we talk of rocks we mean the more solid parts of the Earth's crust.

Rocks fall into three main classes. It is important to classify them not only in order to name them correctly but also to understand how each rock is related to others and how the Earth's rock-forming systems work together to produce such a variety of rock types.

The primary rocks are those formed from molten material, which may be erupted on to the Earth's surface through a volcanic vent as lava, or crystallized deep underground from magma. Both lava and magma are referred to as silicate melts. Deep below the surface – possibly far more than 30km (19 miles) – this silicate melt exists under great pressure and at a temperature well in excess of 1000°C (1832°F). As some of it rises upwards it may become concentrated in a particular part of the Earth's crust, where it gradually solidifies and freezes into a large bloated mass many tens of kilometres in diameter. These masses are called batholiths and are often found in the roots of fold mountain chains such as the Andes and Rockies.

Large masses of magma, because of their size and depth, cool very slowly, sometimes taking 50 million years or more to freeze completely. This slow cooling allows large crystals to form, and attractive rocks like granite, much used for bank and office-block frontages, result. Smaller masses of magma may find weaknesses such as joint and fault lines in the Earth's crust. Narrow vertical sheets of magma invade these weaknesses, forming dykes and horizontal offshoots, called sills. Because these cool higher in the crust (they are hypabyssal intrusions as opposed to the plutonic batholiths) they freeze quite rapidly and the resulting rocks have a medium-grained texture (a grain diameter of 0.5–5mm). Dolerite is a typical example.

The term 'texture' refers to the size and shape of the grains and their inter-relationship. In the igneous rocks, texture depends

Below: *The grain size of igneous rocks is determined by where they cool. Their chemistry depends on their origin. Basic rocks (right) come from the deepest parts of the crust, where they begin as gabbro. Dolerite occurs in smaller masses higher up and erupted lava takes the form of basalt. Acid rocks (left) are formed in the upper crust. Granite is in the magma chamber, micro-granite occurs in smaller masses and rhyolite is erupted. Intermediate igneous rocks are diorite at depth, micro-diorite in the offshoots and andesite as lava.*

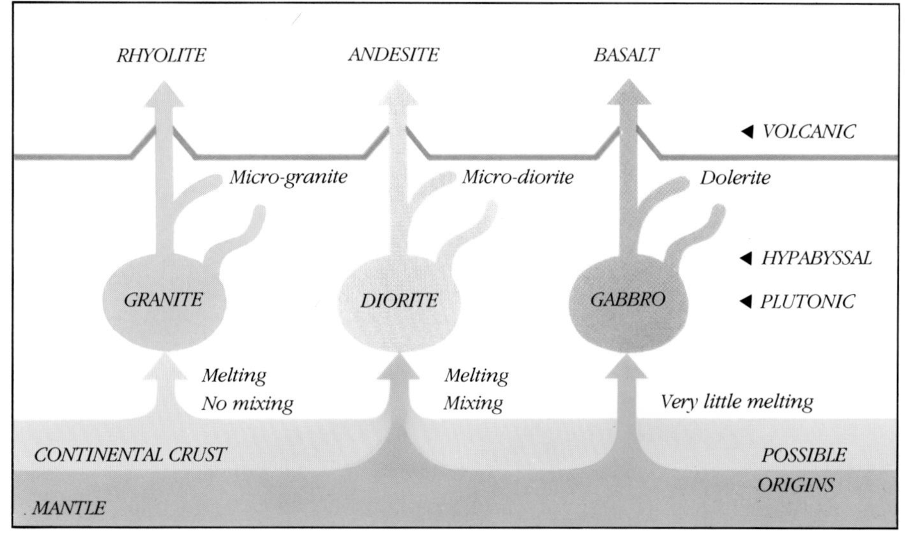

Below: *Large igneous intrusions (upper diagram) form a variety of structures, from saucer-shaped lopoliths to huge batholiths and smaller plutons. Minor intrusions (lower diagram) usually occur as sheets, either cutting across existing strata or following bedding planes and other structures. Concordant sills lie along existing planes; dykes, which are discordant, cut across earlier structures. Sheet intrusions are often associated with volcanic activity. Cone sheets and ring dykes usually lie below volcanoes.*

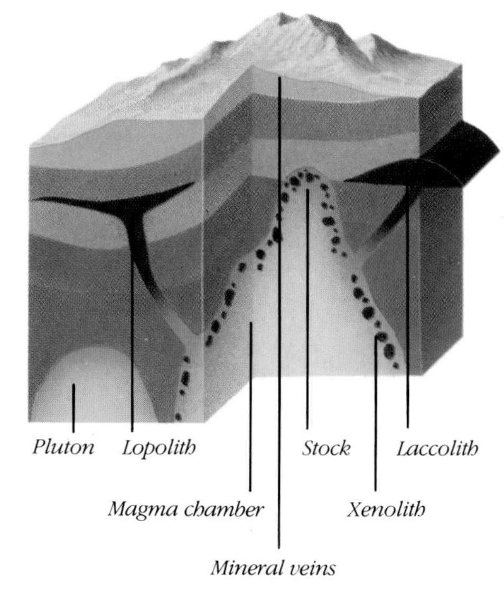

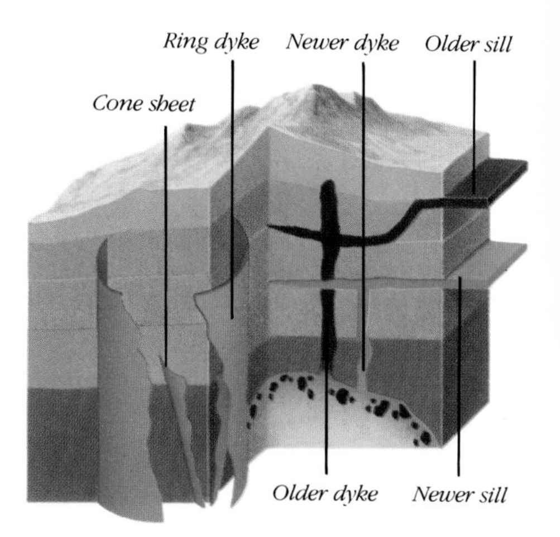

Left: *Pillow lava. When lava is erupted on the sea bed, the outer surface, in contact with cold sea water, quickly solidifies, forming a skin around still-molten rock. The lava continues to move, causing the formation of pillow shapes. These pillow lavas, on the coast of Anglesey, North Wales, were formed in the Pre-Cambrian era. Such structures have been observed forming on today's ocean bed by using remote sensing techniques.*

very largely on what is referred to as the cooling history of the rock. The main aspects of this are the time taken for cooling to occur and whether there have been interruptions and changes in the speed of cooling. If, for example, there have been two distinct stages in the cooling of magma, an attractive rock texture called porphyritic texture develops. Here there are large crystals (phenocrysts) set into a relatively finer matrix. What may have happened is that the magma began cooling slowly, possibly at a considerable depth in the crust. This allowed certain minerals to grow to a large size within the liquid magma. The magma then moved to a much higher level in the crust, or may even have been erupted on to the surface, and the rock matrix froze rapidly, with resulting small grain size, enveloping the already-formed large crystals.

When magma reaches the surface it becomes lava. Depending on the chemical properties of the lava, it may erupt with great violence or well out slowly and cover huge areas without forming a characteristic steep volcanic cone. The lavas which are silica-rich have great explosive power, while those with lower silica content are less viscous and erupt gently. Rhyolite and andesite make for violent volcanoes, resulting in steep-sided cones, while basalt lava, being very runny, produces large, flat volcanic shields.

The various lavas are fine-grained rocks because of rapid cooling, but they also exhibit some interesting textural features. Lavas are, for example, often rich in gases. As lava solidifies the gas bubbles are released, leaving behind them rounded hollows called vesicles. These vesicular lavas provide good sites for minerals to form at a later time, possibly millions of years after the lava itself has frozen. When the vesicles have been infilled with rounded patches of minerals (quartz, calcite and zeolites are common), the term amygdaloidal (almond-shaped) is used. Lavas are often erupted on the sea bed, and when this happens a skin freezes around the still molten lava mass. The molten lava continues to move and stretch this skin, giving the appearance of a rounded sack or pillow. Such pillow lavas, often with siliceous chert in the rounded gaps between them, are very characteristic of underwater eruptions.

Overall grain size, determined by cooling speed, is one of the two parameters on which the identification and classification of igneous rocks are based. The other criterion is their chemistry. This is understood by considering mineral content. The acid rocks contain a high percentage (over 65 per cent) of total silica and over 10 per cent quartz. The intermediate rocks contain less silica at 55–65 per cent, while the basic rocks have only 45–55 per cent. The ultra-basic rocks contain less than 45 per cent. Acid rocks are generally pale in colour and contain feldspar and mica as well as quartz, whereas basic rocks are dark and heavy with feldspar, pyroxene and little quartz. Intermediate rocks have some characteristics of both basic and acid rocks, while the very heavy ultra-basic rocks are often virtually mono-mineralic, being made of ferromagnesian minerals such as olivine, pyroxene and amphibole.

Below: *Types of volcanic eruption.* **1** *Fissure eruptions produce the greatest flows of basic runny lava.* **2** *Hawaiian eruptions produce a less fluid lava and build up low-angled volcanoes that often contain a lava lake.* **3** *Strombolian activity is more violent. Fire fountains of red-hot ash build a cone, often breached by lava flows.* **4** *Surtseyan cones, with wide craters and low walls, form when water reacts explosively with molten rock.* **5** *Plinian eruptions, the most violent, are gas blasts that reach immense heights and throw out a mass of material.*

ACID IGNEOUS ROCKS

These contain over 65 per cent total silica and they are characteristically pale-coloured, low-density rocks, with over 10 per cent quartz as well as both orthoclase and plagioclase feldspars and the various types of mica. Hornblende is not uncommon and iron pyrites may be an accessory mineral. Granite is one of the most abundant igneous rocks in the continental crust and forms enormous batholiths in many mountain chains. In Peru and in British Columbia, Canada, for example, there are granitic batholiths stretching over 1600km (994 miles) in length and 190km (118 miles) in width. In Britain the batholith in the south-west peninsula extends beneath much of Devon and Cornwall, reaching out into the Atlantic at the Scilly Isles.

Granite

As a typical acid rock, granite may contain well over 30 per cent quartz, orthoclase and plagioclase, the last of which is usually sodium-rich. Granites commonly have more orthoclase than plagioclase but sometimes the amounts of plagioclase and orthoclase are equal, in which case the rock is called adamellite. Granite rocks frequently have a speckled appearance because of the presence of black or brown mica, usually biotite. White muscovite mica is also common and dark hornblende may add to the speckled appearance. Other minerals, such as sphene and apatite, can also occur, and the variety of detail in the chemistry of granites gives rise to many types within the general category of coarse-grained and acidic. The texture is often equigranular, crystals being of equal size. Porphyritic texture is, however, quite common, and some of the most attractive ornamental granites have this texture with large feldspar crystals set in a matrix of quartz, feldspar and mica. The phenocrysts can grow to over 5cm (2in) in length, but when the whole rock has grains over 3cm (1¼in) long, the term pegmatite is used.

Many granites have a magmatic origin, as is witnessed by their crystalline nature, the thermal metamorphism of the adjacent

Right: *Granite. Note the coarse texture and random orientation of minerals. The pinkish crystals of orthoclase feldspar are about 1cm (½in) long and give the rock a porphyritic texture. The matrix is of black biotite mica and white feldspar with some grey quartz.*

country rock and the inclusion of xenoliths (blocks of country rock caught up in the magma and altered). However, some granitic bodies may originate from very high-grade regional metamorphism, in the process of which the presence of high-temperature fluids, as well as pressure and temperature conditions, can alter any rocks and produce a rock chemically very like granite though structurally rather different. Such granitized rocks may have a hazy outline in the field, with areas of migmatite surrounding them.

Pegmatite

Pegmatites are very coarse granitic rocks containing some of the largest crystals in the Earth's crust. These rocks are associated with the ultimate stages of the crystallization of a magma body, and because of this they often contain the minerals formed from rare elements such as tungsten and radioactive materials. The main minerals in pegmatites are very similar to those in granites and other acid igneous rocks. There is usually much mica and quartz, and orthoclase feldspar is in abundance, giving some pegmatite bodies a bright pink colour (see the photograph on page 5). As well as large crystals formed of these essential minerals, pegmatites contain large crystals of accessories such as beryl, tourmaline, fluorite and rutile – specimens over 15m (49ft) long have been found. Around the margins of granitic masses, veins and dykes of pegmatite may occur.

Above: *A pegmatite dyke. Composed almost entirely of pink orthoclase feldspar, with some quartz, this dyke is 60cm (2ft) wide and cuts through contorted gneisses on the north-west coast of Scotland. Its discordant nature is well displayed. Pegmatites often occur as small intrusions of this kind.*

Micro-granite

The term micro-granite or quartz-porphyry is used for the medium-grained acid rocks. These are chemically the same as their coarser-grained relatives but have a medium grain size because of their occurrence in minor intrusions such as sills and dykes.

Rhyolite

Rhyolites are acid lavas. These extremely hard, pale-coloured flinty lavas are erupted with great violence from steep-sided volcanic cones and are often associated with frothy gas cloud eruptions called *nuées ardentes*. These eruptions produce a welded rhyolitic tuff named ignimbrite. Rhyolitic tuff consists of numerous acid lava particles welded together in a siliceous matrix. If such particles settle in water the rock will be neatly bedded, but rhyolites often show a wavy flow banding structure rather than bedding of this type. Although rhyolites are chemically similar to granites they are often richer in quartz, but in any case they are so fine-grained that the crystals in them are difficult to see even with a microscope.

Left: *Rhyolite. Pale phenocrysts of feldspar (1mm/¹/₂₅in long) give this specimen its porphyritic texture. The fine-grained matrix has the same composition as granite. The phenocrysts probably crystallized beneath the surface and were solid crystals at the time of eruption. The matrix formed around them on the surface.*

Obsidian

This is a very rapidly cooled acidic lava, usually very dark in colour and with a glassy texture. It has a conchoidal fracture and breaks with sharp edges. This rock is common in lava flow erupted from acidic volcanoes, a famous example being Obsidian Cliff in Yellowstone National Park in the USA.

INTERMEDIATE IGNEOUS ROCKS

Intermediate igneous rocks fall chemically between the acid and basic ones. They are at times difficult rocks to define and identify, but they do have a number of characteristics which are a useful guide. They contain less than 10 per cent quartz, and many contain both plagioclase and alkali feldspar (potassium/sodium feldspar). Sometimes only plagioclase may be present, in which case it is usually in the form of andesine or oligoclase, both of which are towards the centre of the plagioclase series. Ferro-magnesian minerals are also present, hornblende being common in rocks like diorite and syenite, along with biotite and pyroxene. Though this is only a general guide, the intermediate rocks are darker in overall colour than the acid rocks, but not as dark as the basic ones. The total silica content of the intermediate rocks is between 55 and 65 per cent.

Syenite

This is a coarse-grained intermediate rock which in some respects is similar to granite in general appearance, often with a speckled grey or pink overall colouring. The texture may be porphyritic or pegmatitic, but is usually equigranular. The essential minerals are alkali feldspar or plagioclase (sometimes both) and amphibole or pyroxene, and also biotite mica. Quartz can be present, but here syenite differs greatly from granite in that the former contains less than 10 per cent of this mineral.

A great many types of syenite have been named. Nepheline syenite contains the feldspathoid nepheline. (Feldspathoids are silicate minerals with potassium or sodium or both in their structure.) Quartz syenite contains about 10 per cent quartz, but above this figure it grades into granite. Syenites occur in sills and dykes and in larger discordant intrusions of plutonic origin, but these are generally much smaller than the masses formed by granites.

Micro-syenite

This is similar in its chemistry to syenite, but has medium-sized crystals. It is often porphyritic and many types with this texture are known from Scandinavia. These are called rhomb porphyry and are found as glacial erratics (that is, boulders deposited by Ice Age glaciers) on the east coast of England. Micro-syenite contains some quartz, alkali

Below: *Micro-syenite. With a medium-grained matrix, this porphyritic syenite has the composition of a typical intermediate rock, with feldspars, amphibole, mica and pyroxene. There is less than 10% quartz. The feldspar phenocrysts are about 1cm (½in) long.*

Above: *Andesite. This specimen from the volcano Poas, Costa Rica, has a vesicular texture, being full of small gas bubble cavities. The mineralogy is impossible to deduce from a hand specimen, even with a lens, but in this sample there are some pale pyroxene phenocrysts.*

feldspar, pyroxene, hornblende and biotite. The phenocrysts, which may show a flow texture, are usually feldspar. This rock is found in minor intrusions such as sills and dykes.

Diorite

Another rock with a speckled appearance, diorite is coarse- or medium-grained, often with a porphyritic texture, and with a mineralogy similar to that of syenite. There is less than 10 per cent quartz, and plagioclase with ferromagnesians, such as biotite, and either hornblende or pyroxene make up the bulk of the rock matrix. Accessory minerals include magnetite, sphene and apatite. This mineralogy is very different from that of dolerite or gabbro (basic rocks) which have a similar overall appearance. Diorite is found in small intrusions and around the margins of larger ones, where the diorite rock gradually changes into the main coarser-grained intrusion rock.

Andesite

This is one of the intermediate volcanic rocks. As lava it cooled rapidly and so is fine-grained. Andesite is often porphyritic, indicating that some minerals froze while the lava was underground and these crystals were carried out in the lava, which then solidified around them. It contains less than 10 per cent quartz with plagioclase, pyroxene, amphibole and biotite. These rocks may be amygdaloidal or vesicular, and when they have frozen very rapidly they have a glassy texture. Andesite is a rock from explosive volcanoes and is therefore similar to rhyolite in occurrence, though it is usually darker in colour.

Trachyte

Another intermediate lava is trachyte, which gives its name to a flow texture of minerals – trachitic – in which feldspars are aligned parallel to one another. Trachyte has a composition similar to that of syenite.

BASIC IGNEOUS ROCKS

Basic igneous rocks are dark in colour and tend to be of higher relative density than the acid and intermediate rocks. Basaltic rocks have a density of about 3.3. In terms of surface area covered, basalt is one of the commonest rocks in the crust as it forms the floors of the oceans. The basic rocks have fewer minerals in them than the acid and intermediate rocks, usually being composed of feldspar (plagioclase), pyroxene and olivine, with a small percentage (less than 10 per cent) of quartz. Biotite mica, hornblende and iron oxide (magnetite) can be present in very small amounts. The total silica content is 45–55 per cent.

Gabbro

This is a coarse-grained plutonic basic rock. It is generally dark-coloured, but it has a surface which is mottled with white and black or very dark green crystals. The plagioclase contained in gabbro tends to be calcium-rich (anorthite). The darker crystals are pyroxene (often augite), and paler green olivine, a ferro-magnesian material, may also be visible. Rock with significant amounts of olivine is known as olivine gabbro. The texture of gabbro is usually equigranular, but ophitic texture, in which feldspar crystals are surrounded by pyroxene, is not uncommon. Gabbro forms in intrusions of considerable size which are often complex and sheet-shaped. These masses may be layered, as in the Skaergaard complex in Greenland.

Dolerite

The medium-grained equivalent of gabbro tends to occur in minor intrusions. It is probably the commonest rock in sills and dykes. The latter may occur in swarms of many hundreds in some parts of the Earth's crust, for example the Inner Hebrides off the west coast of Scotland. Because of its medium grain size, the minerals in dolerite are not easy to detect in detail unless a hand lens is used. Without a lens the rock simply has a speckled dark and light appearance. The minerals contained are plagioclase (pale coloured), pyroxene (dark) and possibly

Right: *Similar in composition to gabbro, medium-grained and speckled in appearance, dolerite is found in minor intrusions. This photograph was shot at the same magnification as the one of gabbro, allowing comparison.*

Left: *Gabbro. Basic rocks contain two main minerals, clearly seen in this coarse-grained specimen. The pale crystals are plagioclase feldspar and the dark green prismatic crystals, up to 1cm (½in) long, are pyroxene.*

olivine, magnetite and less than 10 per cent quartz. When weathered, dolerite forms very characteristic spheroidal shapes, with 'onion-skin' layers around them. Columnar jointing, where hexagonal or polygonal joints develop in the cooling magma, is common in dolerite intrusions. In sills the jointing is vertical, at right angles to the cooling surfaces, and in dykes this structure is horizontal. Where sills of some thickness are present (many tens of metres), there may be a variation in the detailed composition vertically through the intrusion. Near the base a layer rich in olivine may form, because olivine, one of the first minerals to freeze, has sunk through the liquid magma before other minerals formed. The rest of such an intrusion will be dolerite while the composition of this lowest part may approach that of an ultra-basic rock.

Basalt

Lava of basic composition is called basalt. It is a very fluid non-viscous lava and flows for great distances before finally freezing, often forming broad, gently sloping volcanic cones like those in Hawaii and Iceland. It has a high gas content and therefore the rock formed is often very vesicular. The gas bubble cavities may be filled at a later stage in the rock's history to become amygdales, which may contain a variety of minerals including zeolites, calcite and quartz, although these minerals have no bearing on the rock's chemistry. When quartz occurs in the vesicles it may be in the form of agate.

Basalt contains calcium-rich plagioclase feldspar, pyroxene, olivine and some quartz, with magnetite as a common accessory. Indeed, the magnetite contained in the basalts which form the ocean bed have been used to prove the theory of sea floor spreading by a study of their reversed and non-reversed magnetic patterns. The crystals in basalt can only be seen properly with a microscope slide (see pages 6–7); in a hand specimen the rock is dark and fine-grained. Basalt can be porphyritic, the phenocrysts being euhedral and not rounded like the amygdales.

Below: *Basalt. Note the dark, shiny nature of the fresh rock and its vesicular texture (with many small gas bubble cavities). The grain size is so fine that no crystals can be detected.*

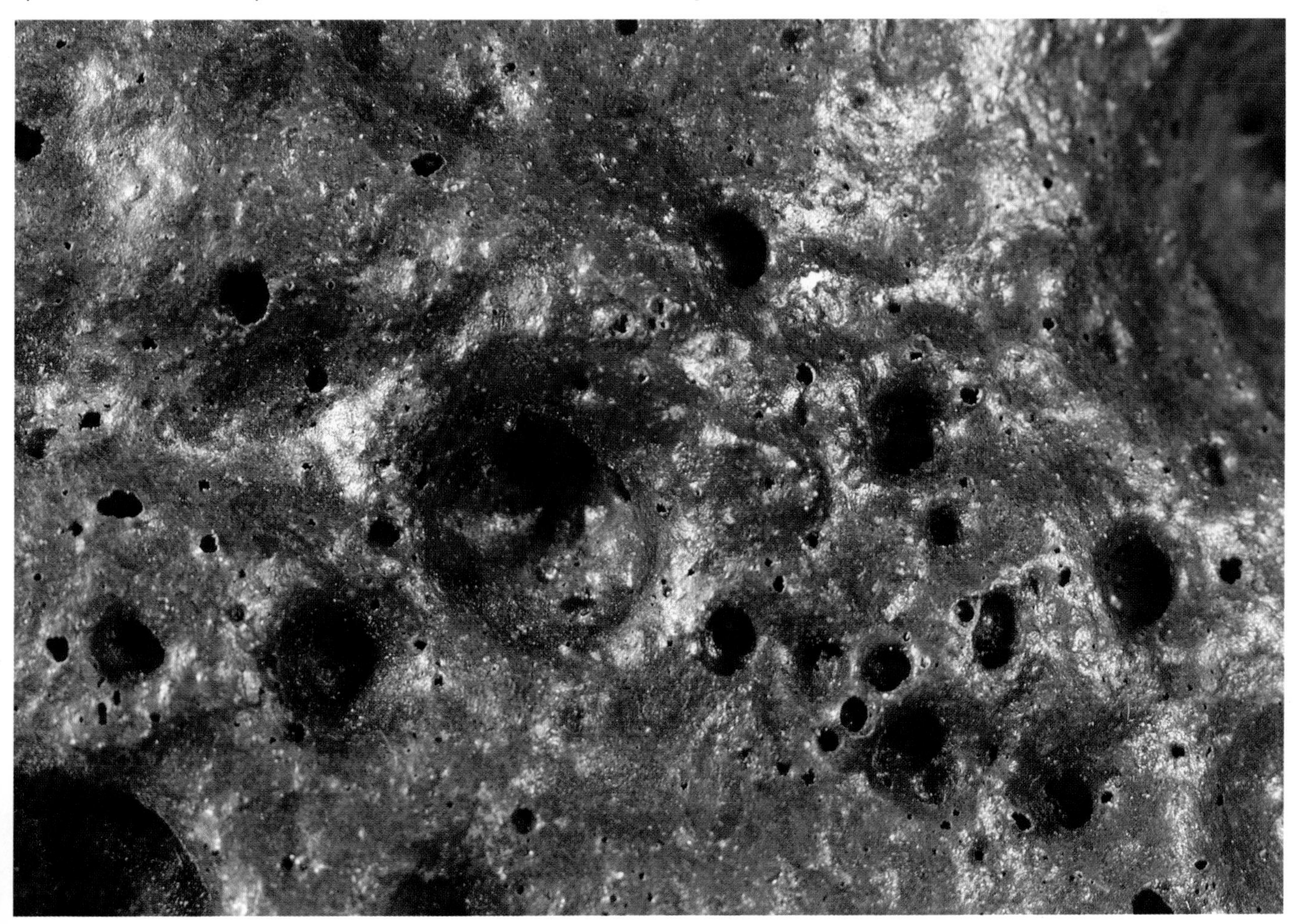

ULTRA-BASIC IGNEOUS ROCKS

The ultra-basic igneous rocks are those which are very low in their total silica content. Quartz is therefore usually absent, as are the lower-density silicates like feldspars and feldspathoids. The main minerals found in these rocks are the ferromagnesians, such as olivine, pyroxene and amphibole. In some cases the rock may be made almost entirely of one of these minerals and classified according to mineral content, with names such as hornblendite, pyroxenite and olivinite, although dunite is the name commonly applied to olivine-rich ultra-basic rock.

Ultra-basic rocks are of high density and are very dark in colour (ultra-mafic). Their composition is not very different from that of rock which is thought to be present in the upper parts of the Earth's mantle and the very deepest parts of the crust. The most common ultra-basic rocks are found in plutonic masses, although occasionally minor intrusions, such as sills and dykes, are composed of this rock type. In the general scheme of igneous rock classification, ultra-basic rocks are categorized as containing less than 45 per cent total silica. However, this rather precise demarcation does not work in all cases, as some rocks which on all other counts are ultra-basic may contain as much as 50 per cent total silica.

Peridotite is the commonest variety of plutonic ultra-basic rock. Picrite is another kind, of which there are some fine-grained varieties. It is composed of about 10 per cent feldspar and 90 per cent ferromagnesian minerals and can, with an increase in feldspar content, become similar in composition to gabbro and basalt.

Peridotite

This rock has a coarse-grained, often granular texture and is composed mainly of ferromagnesian minerals. These include olivine, pyroxene and amphibole, though only rarely are all present in the rock. Usually the rock is made almost exclusively of just one of these. Metallic minerals like chromite also occur. The rock is very heavy and dark in colour, usually being black or dark green. Small red or brown patches in the rock are garnet crystals. The origin of peridotite varies. Some masses are xenoliths found in lavas which have dragged blocks of ultra-

Below: *Garnet peridotite. With a dark greenish matrix of amphibole and some olivine, this sample is dotted with red garnet crystals. Garnet peridotite is a heavy rock with a specific gravity of about 3.5. The specimen is from Scotland and Pre-Cambrian in age.*

Right: *Dunite. This ultra-basic rock is composed almost entirely of the ferro-magnesian mineral olivine. This composition accounts for the rock's greenish colour and its granular, sugary texture. The specimen here is 12cm (4¾in) across and is from New Zealand.*

basic rock from the mantle of the Earth. Other occurrences include layers of peridotite in gabbro intrusions and sheet intrusions in Pre-Cambrian basement complexes.

Dunite

A rock composed almost entirely of olivine, this type of peridotite is therefore known as mono-mineralic. It has a granular texture which is often almost sugary. Chromite may be present, as may some hornblende and pyroxene. The colour is unlike that of many other ultra-basic rocks, as dunite may be pale green or brown.

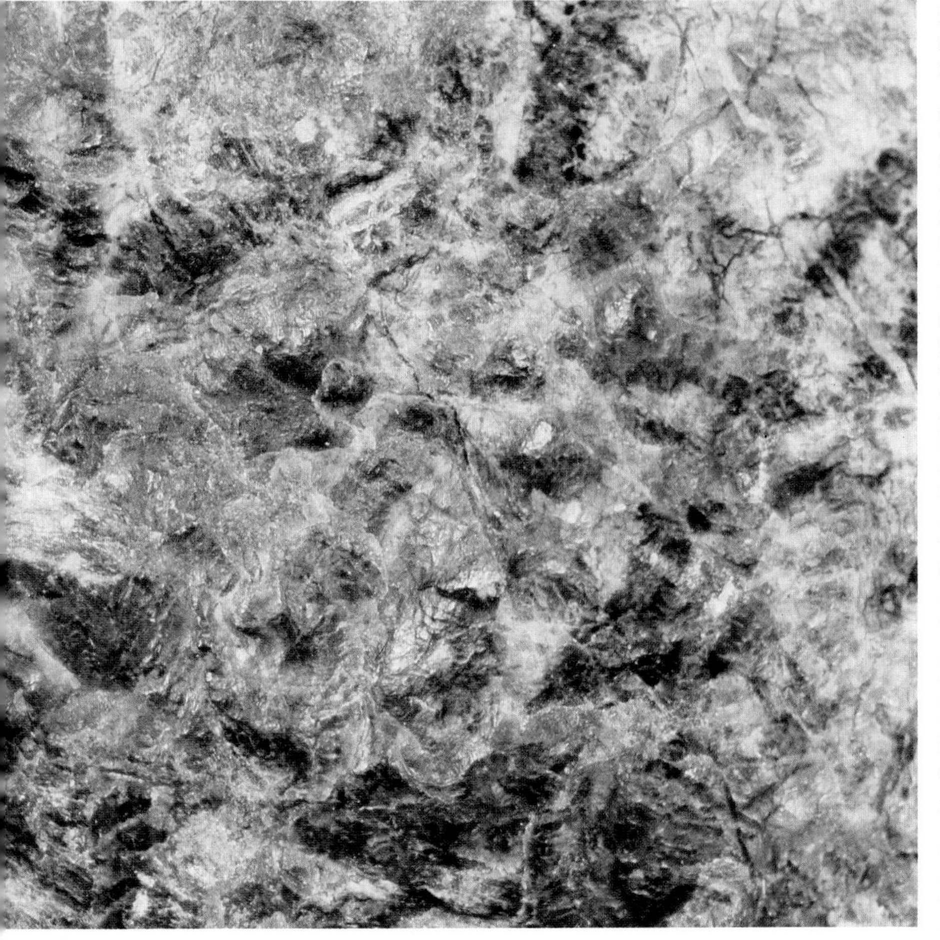

Left: *Red veins running through a greenish matrix are typical of serpentinite's striking appearance. The sample is 9.5cm (3¾in) across.*

Serpentinite

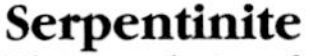

This rock is often classified with the ultra-basic igneous rocks, although some authorities feel it should be included with the metamorphic rocks. It is formed by the alteration of ultra-basic materials, a process which involves the influence of water, producing a rock often of very striking appearance. It is dark-coloured but varies from green to almost black and bright red. These colours may be mingled and cross each other as patches and stripes. The grains are coarse- or medium-sized. The minerals are both those of the original ultra-basic rock, olivine, pyroxene and amphibole, together with those produced by serpentinization, including antigorite and chrysotile. Magnetite is also often present. Serpentinite occurs as discrete masses in areas of metamorphic rocks, and as dykes or other small discordant intrusions.

Pyroxenite

Another virtually mono-mineralic rock, pyroxenite consists mainly of pyroxene. It is dark green in colour, or sometimes brown and black. The grain size is coarse or medium, and it occurs in layers in intrusive bodies, or in separate small intrusions such as sills and dykes. As well as pyroxene, this rock may contain a variety of minerals including hornblende, olivine, chromite, garnet and biotite.

SEDIMENTARY ROCKS

When rocks are exposed on the surface, they may be in an environment very different from that in which they were formed. Temperature and pressure are a fraction of those where the igneous and metamorphic rocks form. The weather plays on these rocks and breaks them down. Granite, for example, often thought of as the essential hard, durable rock, is very susceptible to mechanical and chemical breakdown. Frost exploits its natural joint systems, while the feldspars in granite are chemically altered to clay and the rock then becomes a loose sand. Whatever the original rock, the processes of weathering, erosion and deposition produce this second large class of rocks, the sedimentary rocks.

Sedimentary rocks fall naturally into a number of groups. Those made of weathered and eroded particles are the detrital or fragmentary rocks. Sandstones, shales and conglomerates are in this group, and may exhibit on their bedding planes such features as ripple marks and mud cracks, telling geologists something of the environment in which they were formed. These rocks are for many reasons more easy to interpret than the igneous or metamorphic rocks. The sediments are formed at the Earth's surface, in the environment with which we are familiar, and by applying our knowledge of the Earth's current surface processes to the features of a sedimentary rock we can often reconstruct the type of conditions under which it was formed.

Below: *Stratification. Sedimentary rocks are deposited in distinct layers or strata. Clearly visible in this photograph of a sea cliff in northern Scotland are sandstone strata which, though presumed to have been level when laid down, now dip towards the west (to the left in the photograph). The pale colouring is the result of that part of the cliff being covered by the sea at high tide.*

Below: *Old rock is continuously removed and new strata formed. In hot regions, salt lakes with crystalline evaporites develop, and where rain is too sparse to support plants, dunes form and migrate with the wind. Under the sea, turbid slurries of sediment are funnelled through canyons in the continental slope, carrying material onto the deep ocean bed.*

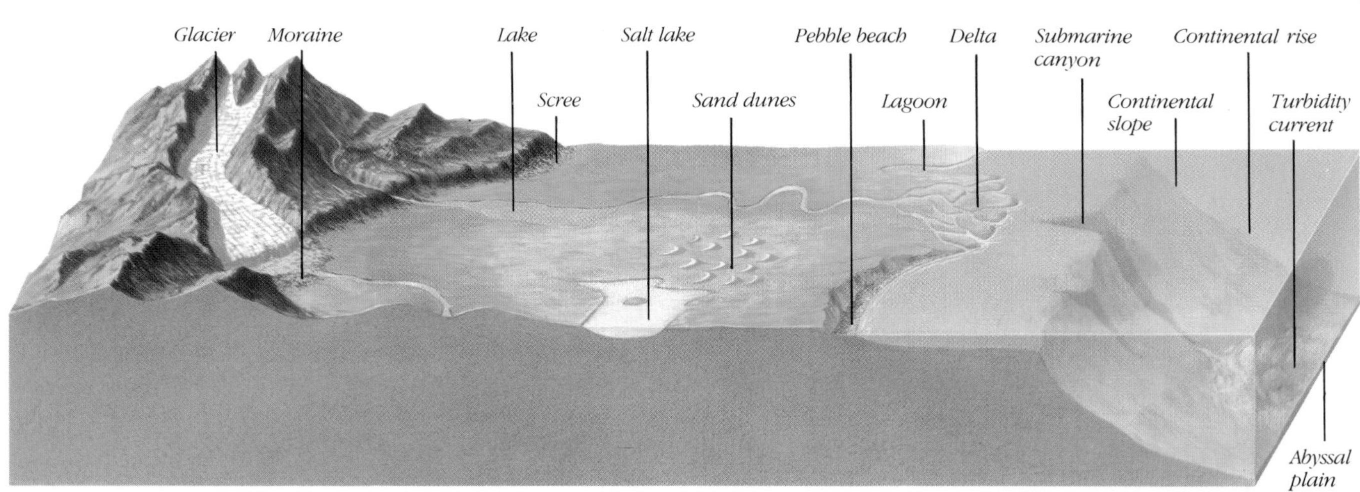

Other sediments include the limestones, some of which are deposited organically as reefs of biological material or the accumulations of millions of tiny fossils, as in that unique powdery limestone, chalk. Others may be the result of chemical activity on the sea bed, causing lime or dolomite to form solid rock material. Because of their susceptibility to chemical weathering the limestones produce some of the most striking landscapes in the world, often called Karst landscape after the area of Yugoslavia where such terrain is well known. Further sediments include coals and ironstones, both of great economic significance, as are the evaporite deposits of rock salt, gypsum and potash.

The main feature which brings this great variety of sedimentary rocks together is that they are all deposited in layers or beds (strata) which initially are reasonably flat and well organized. Subsequently these strata may be folded and faulted by movements in the crust. Many of their initial characteristics are of great use in helping geologists find out if the strata are the correct way up and in sequence.

Below: *Sandstone. The angular grains of this medium-grained rock are mainly of quartz, with some rock fragments and pinkish feldspar, and 1–2mm (1/25–1/12in) in diameter. Iron oxide and feldspar give the red colour.*

DETRITAL SEDIMENTS

Sandstone

One of the best known of the detrital sedimentary rocks, this is made of grains of medium size which vary in their shape according to the depositional environment. For example, sand grains in desert regions have a characteristically rounded shape, whereas those in water-lain sediments tend to be more angular. The grains themselves are largely quartz, but other minerals, such as feldspar and mica, can also be present. (The rock is called arkose when it contains more than 25 per cent feldspar.) The grains can be held together by minerals which have been formed in the pore spaces in the rock, and these include calcite, iron oxides and quartz. Often sandstones are said to be well sorted, which means that the grains are all about the same size. Bedding structures and other sedimentary features are well displayed in these rocks, though fossils are not always common.

Conglomerate and breccia

These coarse-grained rocks are very variable and are made of large fragments, both of minerals (often quartz) and rocks from the source area. In conglomerates these fragments are rounded, indicating the influence of water during erosion and transportation, but in the closely related rock breccia there are angular fragments. Conglomerates are often found just above an unconformity, where they may represent beach deposits or the strata formed by river systems.

Shale

Along with clay and mudstone, shale makes up the group of fine-grained detrital sedimentary rocks. Shales are often deposited in very neat, thin beds and contain minerals such as quartz, mica and clay minerals. Some dark-coloured shales contain carbon and finely scattered iron pyrites. Fossils are often very well preserved in shales, sometimes as flattened impressions, but occasionally in discrete nodules made of iron pyrites or calcareous material.

Shales may develop from clays as the rocks are buried and compacted in the Earth's crust. These fine-grained rocks tend to be formed in deeper water than sandstones and conglomerates, because the fine particles are easily carried by water currents.

Below: *Shales are extremely fine-grained sedimentary rocks, being made up of grains which are too small to be picked out with the naked eye. They are rocks in which fossils are often very well preserved. The specimen in the photograph is of Lower Jurassic age and contains many crushed ammonites of the genus* Harpoceras.

LIMESTONES

The classification of limestones distinguishes between those formed by or from organic material (shelly limestone, coral limestone and algal limestone), those originating from chemical activity (such as oolite and dolomitic limestones) and those formed from fragments of calcareous material (clastic limestones). The predominant minerals are calcite and dolomite, and some varieties also contain a low percentage of siderite (iron carbonate). Although limestones can be deposited in fresh water, the vast majority are marine deposits, commonly formed in a reasonably clear sea, largely free of mud and sand.

Limestones contain abundant fossils but, because limestones recrystallize rapidly and easily during diagenesis, the fossils may be lost, along with sedimentary features which would have been of great value when trying to deduce the environment of deposition. The older the limestone formation, the more likely this is. These rocks are usually pale-coloured, being grey or even white, though the colour will depend on the amount of detrital material present. They may be a brownish colour when iron minerals are present, and almost black if there is much mud and organic carbon in them.

Limestone is of great economic significance, being used as a building material and in the cement-making industry, and as a flux in steel-making. It is a rock which is therefore quarried in great quantities, often leaving huge, unsightly scars on the landscape. Because of the special characteristics of this rock and the chemical weathering to which it is prone, the limestone landscape is most striking. Limestone soils often support rare flora and fauna, another reason for care when economic exploitation is considered.

Organic limestone

This is a general term for limestone rocks which are rich in fossils, not only of shelled creatures but also of crinoids, corals and other organisms. The different types are, however, given special names. Crinoidal limestone, for example, is made of broken stems of crinoids (organisms related to

Below: *Organic limestone. This specimen consists of numerous fossils of Silurian age – trilobites, bryzoans and brachiopods – cemented in a fine lime mud matrix. The rock was probably formed under quite shallow marine conditions, probably on a continental shelf.*

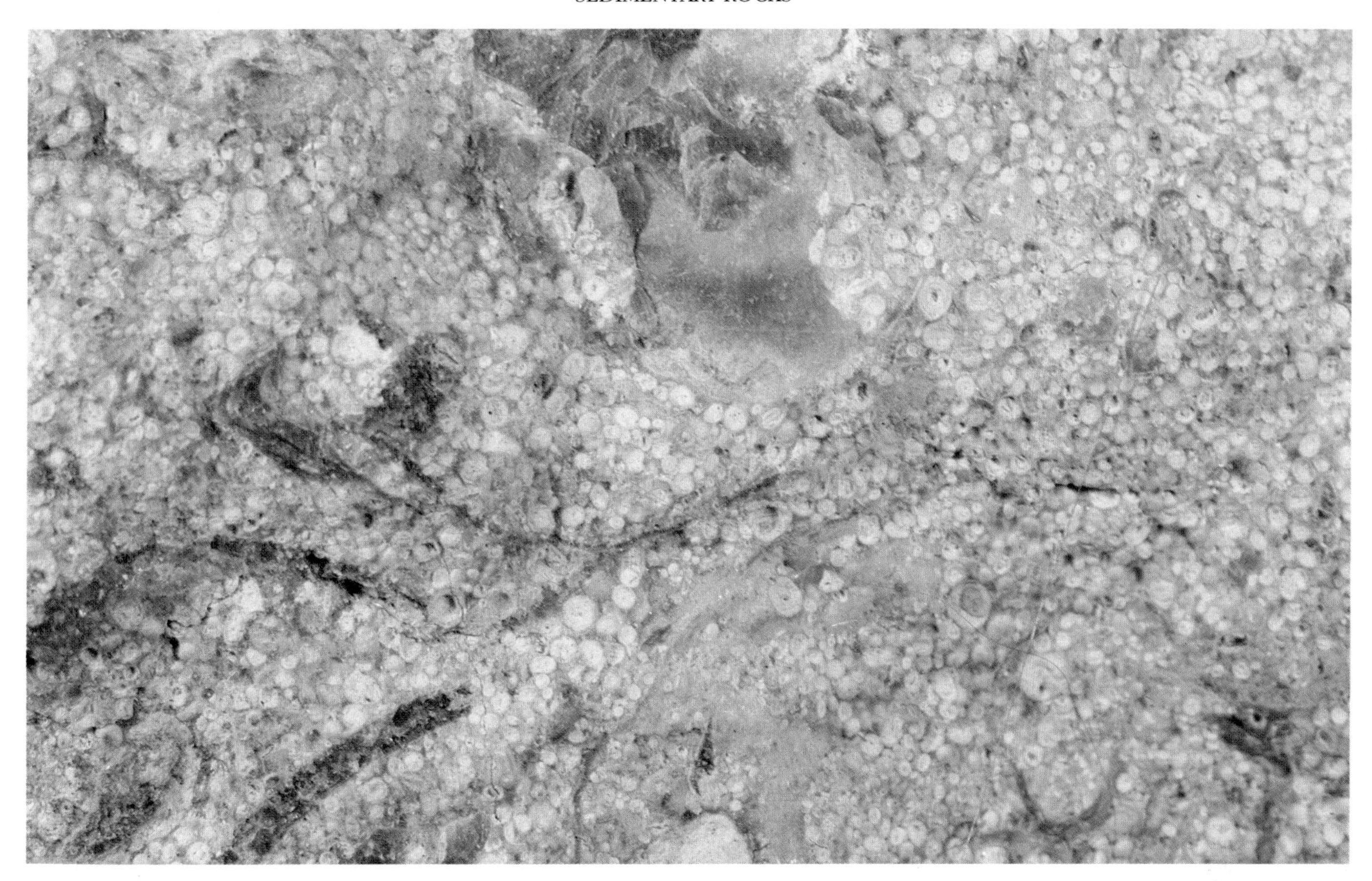

Above: *Oolitic limestone. Of Jurassic age, this specimen shows the small, rounded ooliths in the calcite matrix. Note the concentrically layered structure where the ooliths are broken. The long and flat grey objects are fossil shells.*

starfish and sea urchins), cemented in a calcite matrix. Shelly limestones may have a similar overall appearance but will contain other fossils. The specimen in the photograph shows the remains of trilobites and brachiopods. As well as calcite, these rocks usually contain some detrital quartz and mud. The nature of the fossil content is often a reasonable indication of the conditions in which the rock was deposited and will, for example, indicate if the limestone is marine or fresh-water in origin.

Oolitic limestone

Composed of many small, rounded, calcareous grains, this limestone is quite easy to recognize. These grains (ooliths) are about 1mm in diameter and are cemented in a calcite matrix. When seen with magnification their layered structure, rather like the skins on an onion, is revealed. These calcite layers accumulate around a sand grain or shell fragment. It is believed that this structure is a result of constant movement of the sediment by water currents, probably in shallow, warm seas. Such sediments are accumulating today around the Bahamas. Oolitic limestones are often rich in a great variety of fossils, and they are commonly a pale cream or buff colour.

Chalk

This is another easily recognized rock. It is the most pure limestone and can contain up to 90 per cent or more calcium carbonate, being composed of millions of fossilized micro-organisms, usually *Foraminifera* or coccoliths, cemented in hardened lime mud. The most fascinating feature of the chalk of Cretaceous age found in Britain and Europe is the almost complete lack of detrital material. This has been explained by the theory that any nearby land areas were low-lying and arid. The rock is similar in composition to the oceanic muds found in modern deep-water environments, but the chalk was probably formed in water around 200m (656 ft) deep. It contains many macro-fossils, such as molluscs, brachiopods and echinoderms.

Dolomite

The limestones containing over 15 per cent magnesium carbonate are called dolomites. The term magnesian limestone is also frequently used. These rocks are thought usually to form as a result of the alteration (dolomitization) of pre-formed limestones. This happens through the reaction of brines trapped in the rock with the calcite in the limestone. Often a recrystallization of this type removes fossils and other original structures. Dolomites can also form in evaporite sequences. These rocks are not unlike many other limestones, but tend to be a brownish colour, are often jointed and have widely spaced bedding planes.

EVAPORITES & IRONSTONES

Evaporite sediments are formed in very particular environments. These are often arid regions where a gulf or small arm of the sea has become separated from the main body of sea water. This could be the result of deposition of coastal sediment, for example a bar, or the lowering of sea level. In this now land-locked basin, salts become concentrated as evaporation of the water takes place and chemical precipitation occurs, forming often quite thick layers of evaporite salts. Depending on their solubility in water, there is a definite sequence of deposition. The least soluble minerals, such as calcite and dolomite, will be formed first and therefore will be the oldest layers in a given sequence. These are followed by gypsum and anhydrite, rock salt and finally potash. Not all evaporite sequences contain all these minerals, but there is often cyclic deposition, indicating that the basin has dried up a number of times after successive influxes of marine water. Along with the precipitated layers, there are also beds of mudstone, marl, limestone and sandstone. Thick evaporite sequences occur in many parts of the world.

Rock salt

This term is used for thick, stratified deposits of halite. A common evaporite, rock salt is easily identified. It is usually an orange to brown colour, though in its pure form it is very pale. When clay and other impurities are present it may be dark grey or black. The salty taste is a good way of identifying this shiny, easily broken rock. Under great pressure deep in the Earth's crust rock salt becomes plastic and will flow upwards, breaking through and disrupting overlying strata. This produces dome-shaped salt masses. The layers of rock salt are usually distorted, and are often interbedded with marl or shale. In some regions, rock salt and other evaporites are formed in red bed sequences with red-coloured sandstones. These represent inland arid drainage basins, as opposed to marine evaporite formation.

Gypsum rock

This soft, pale-coloured evaporite often occurs as layers among marls and shales. It is usually white or pinkish in colour and, as with rock salt, it becomes distorted during compaction. Within the beds of gypsum rock, a fibrous structure is often visible.

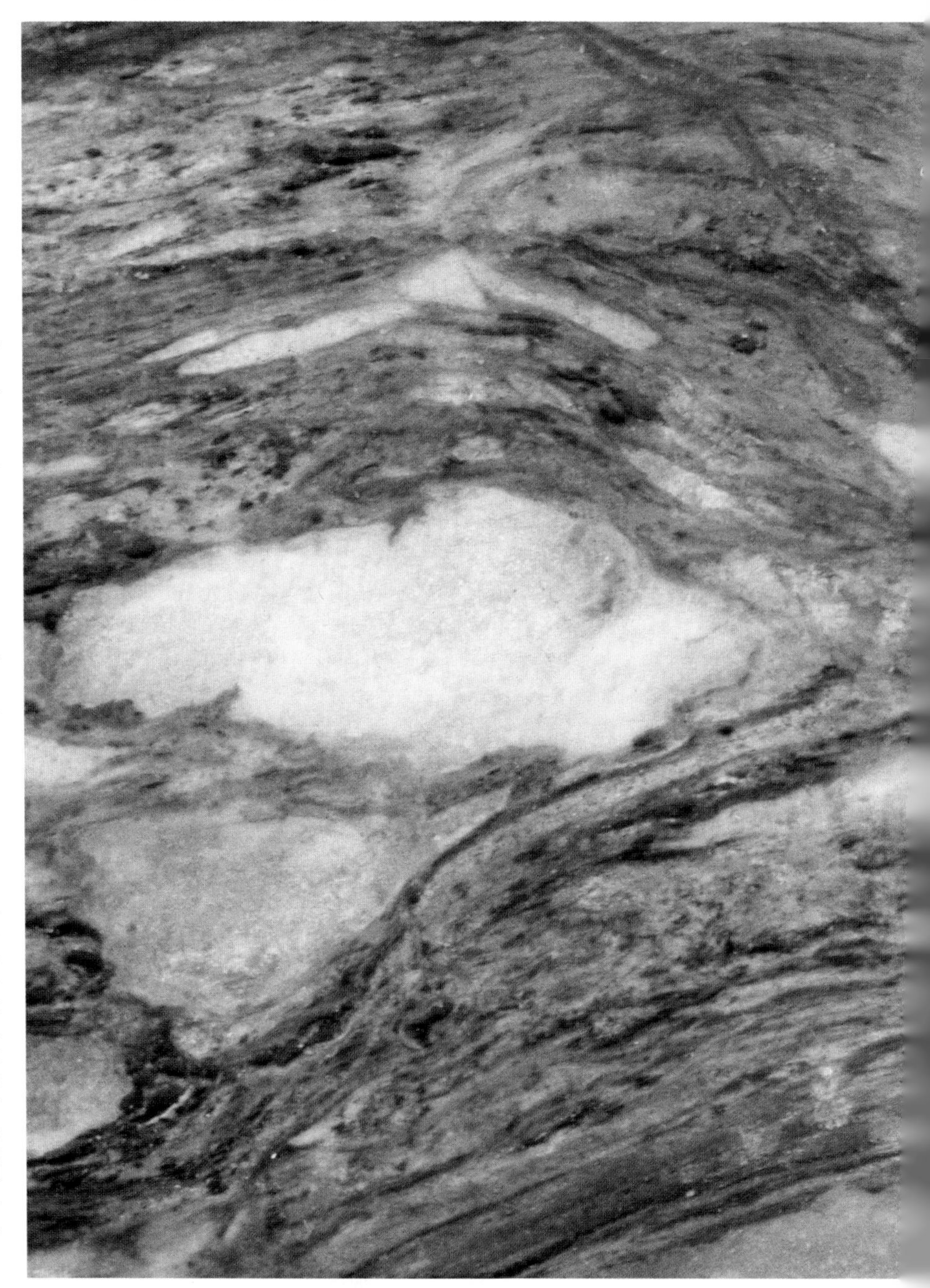

Above: *Gypsum rock. In this specimen, typically contorted layers of gypsum are interbedded with red marl. The white gypsum layers are about 5mm (1/5in) thick. Evaporite deposits are often contorted in this manner because of their ability to flow under pressure.*

Right: *Banded ironstone. A beautiful specimen of this rich ore of iron is shown here, with dark metalliferous bands separated by pinkish quartz. The bands are about 5mm (1/5in) thick. The specimen is from the Pre-Cambrian rocks of the Yilgarn block in Australia.*

Left: *Potash ore, or sylvine. This specimen is shown in close-up so that the bands of reddish potash ore on dark silty marl are clearly visible. The vitreous potash ore is similar in many respects to halite (see Rock salt, opposite, and Halides, p.38), but the two are distinguished from each other by potash ore having a more bitter taste. The specimen in this photograph is 10cm (4in) across.*

Potash ore

Broadly similar to other evaporites, this rock, which is also called sylvine, is not as common as the other varieties. It is often bright red in colour (although in its pure state it is white) and it tastes more bitter than rock salt.

Marl

This sedimentary material is often associated with evaporite deposits. It is a clay-like rock with a high percentage of calcium carbonate in its structure. Marl varies in colour and may be red or green.

Ironstones

Iron minerals occur in a wide variety of sedimentary rocks (and in some igneous rocks) and the accumulation of them in sufficient quantity to make them of economic significance can be a complex process. Many ironstones are of chemical origin, iron-rich solutions finding their way into sediments and possibly replacing minerals already in the rock. This may happen during diagenesis or at a later stage. The minerals involved include chamosite, siderite and limonite; some of the richest ironstones are those containing hematite and magnetite. It is thought that the presence of these minerals may suggest a degree of metamorphic alteration of the iron-bearing strata. Ironstones exhibit many of the typical sedimentary features such as bedding, and are often oolitic. Most ironstones are dark in colour and heavy, although those rich in limonite can be yellowish-brown.

Banded ironstones (see photograph) are rather special in their occurrence and therefore of considerable interest. They are of extreme geological age, usually between 2000 and 3000 million years old. These rocks probably have a very different origin from more recent ironstones, and may have been formed in enclosed basins with an accumulation of iron minerals carried in the very acid waters of the time (when the air was rich in carbon dioxide and the rain was therefore highly acidic).

METAMORPHIC ROCKS

REGIONAL METAMORPHISM

Any rock can be buried to a considerable depth in the crust by movements within the Earth. This usually happens in times of orogeny. These rocks are then in environments of great pressure and temperature, where they become altered and metamorphosed. In addition to these influences, there are very active fluids present at such depth which can add new material to the rock or remove existing minerals. Igneous rocks may withstand certain influences which alter sedimentary rocks; different sediments are altered in different ways and to varying degrees. For example, the conditions which would turn shale or clay into slate have virtually no influence on sandstone, dolerite or granite, although at very high temperature and pressure all rocks undergo metamorphism. Indeed, the trend with metamorphism under the latter conditions is to produce a rock with features more and more like those of an igneous rock as conditions become more extreme. The main difference between an igneous rock and a metamorphic rock is the structure which regional metamorphism creates. Such structure is absent from a magmatic igneous rock. This progressive and widespread type of metamorphism often covers huge areas many tens or hundreds of kilometres across. Slates are the rocks found at the lowest grades, followed by schists and gneisses under progressively more extreme conditions. Much of the Earth's original continental crust is made of gneiss, which is generally the oldest rock in any area.

Above: *Slate. This rock breaks along cleavage planes which develop during metamorphism. In this specimen, the visible surface is a cleavage plane and contains many crystals of iron pyrites, which appear as silvery-yellow cubes. The specimen is 15cm (6in) across.*

Below: *Schist. Dark crystals of biotite mica are clearly visible in this specimen. The surfaces on which these crystals lie are more wavy than the cleavage planes of slate. The specimen measures 15cm (6in) across.*

Slate

This rock is formed in the lowest grade of regional metamorphism. It is often dark-coloured, though green and grey slates are not uncommon. The grains are fine and cannot be picked out with the naked eye. The main feature of slate is its cleavage – that is, the plane along which the rock will easily split because of the new alignment of flaky clay and mica minerals brought about by the pressure influences involved. Structure now determines how the rock will break rather than the original sedimentary bedding. This feature is exploited when slates are split for roofing. Cleavage may be at any angle to the original bedding, and both features are often visible. The other minerals present are quartz and other detritals, as well as some new metamorphic minerals like iron pyrites, as cubes, and chlorite. Slates only form as a result of the weak metamorphism of clays, shales, volcanic tuff and other pelitic rocks.

Schist

This rock is formed at higher pressures and temperatures than slate. The most obvious feature of schists is their foliation or schistosity, a wavy structure running through the rock, produced by the alignment of minerals such as mica, which is very abundant in these rocks. They contain minerals related to the parent rock as well as minerals which develop during metamorphism. The former include quartz and mica, ferro-magnesians and feldspars. The new minerals include chlorite, micas, kyanite and sillimanite, which can be used to study the increasing grade of metamorphism. It has been shown by recent research that temperatures of 300°C (572°F) may be reached in the zone characterized by chlorite and 600°C (1112°F) in the kyanite zone. Pressures of over nine kilobars may exist where schists are formed. Porphyroblasts, discrete crystals set into the fabric of the rock, are common in schists and are often of garnet. Much of the mineralogy depends on that of the original rock; when limestones are metamorphosed at this grade a range of calcsilicate minerals develop, along with diopside, olivine and garnet from the impurities, such as clay, in the limestone. Under these conditions a great many rocks are altered, including most sedimentary and many igneous rocks.

Gneiss

Formed at very deep levels in the crust where the temperature and pressure conditions are extreme and circulating fluids are abundant, gneisses are the ultimate stage in regional metamorphism. Their most characteristic feature is the alternating dark and light bands. The paler ones are rich in quartz and feldspar, while the darker bands contain biotite mica and other ferromagnesian minerals. The rock is coarse-grained and may have a granular texture. Unlike slate and schist, which can be split along the planes of cleavage and foliation, gneiss is a crystalline rock, and the bands do not usually indiate lines along which the rock will split. The banding may often be highly contorted on a local scale, suggesting that the rock was at least plastic while deformation was occurring. Many gneisses have a broadly granitic (acidic) composition; and there is another group of high-grade rocks, eclogites, which are of basic composition. These contain much pyroxene and garnet, and may develop at even greater depth than gneiss. All rocks are altered by the conditions which produce gneiss. Gneisses make up much of the continental shield areas of the Earth's crust and are often of extreme age, being dated at over 3000 million years in some cases.

Above: *Gneiss. The characteristic light and dark bands have been contorted in this specimen, suggesting the rock was plastic during its deformation. It is 1m (39in) across.*

Below: *This table lists the major metamorphic rocks (in the right-hand column) and charts their relationships and origins. You should refer back to it as you read pages 26 and 27.*

Type of Metamorphism	Situation	Main Agents		Rocks before Metamorphism	Rocks after Metamorphism
CONTACT	AUREOLES	HEAT Plus Liquids and Gases		Basalt, Dolerite, Shale, Mudstone, Tuff	HORNFELS
				Sandstone	METAQUARTZITE
				Limestone	MARBLE
REGIONAL	OROGENIC BELTS	PRESSURE Low to High Temperature	Low Temp	Shale, Mudstone, Tuff	SLATE
			Med Temp	Slate, Phyllite, Sandstone, Basalt, Dolerite, Limestone	PHYLLITE, SCHIST
			High Temp and Pressure	All types	GNEISS

CONTACT & DYNAMIC METAMORPHISM

When existing rocks are intruded by magma, or a lava flow runs over them, they are thermally metamorphosed – that is, changed by contact with the magma or lava. Magmas may be at temperatures of over 1000°C (1832°F) and even though metamorphism does not involve melting, great changes occur through contact with such hot material. There is considerable chemical change, though textural features are not nearly as pronounced as in regionally metamorphosed rocks. Limestones are altered to marbles; shales and other pelitic sediments (including volcanic tuffs) may become hornfelses; sandstones are altered to metaquartzites. The area around the igneous rock influenced by high temperature is the metamorphic aureole, and its size depends on the size of the intrusion. A small dyke or sill may have very limited influence, possibly for only 1m (3ft) on either side, but a large batholith may have an aureole many kilometres in width. The type of igneous rock involved also influences the size of the metamorphic aureole; acid magmas, though lower in temperature than basic ones, have more fluids associated with them and so affect the rocks over a wider area. The type of country rock is another factor; the aureole which develops in pelitic sediments is far wider than that in sandstones or igneous rocks, for example.

The third type of metamorphism is dynamic or cataclastic metamorphism, which is brought about by large-scale rock movements such as thrust faults. Rocks are pulverized and metamorphosed within a few metres of where this kind of movement occurs. The new rock produced in this zone is called mylonite, and is characterized by its streaked-out texture and elongated constituents.

Below: *Marble, showing the pale-coloured crystalline nature of metamorphosed limestone and the common dark veining caused by impurities in the original limestone. The greenish colours are olivine crystals. The specimen is 10cm (4in) across.*

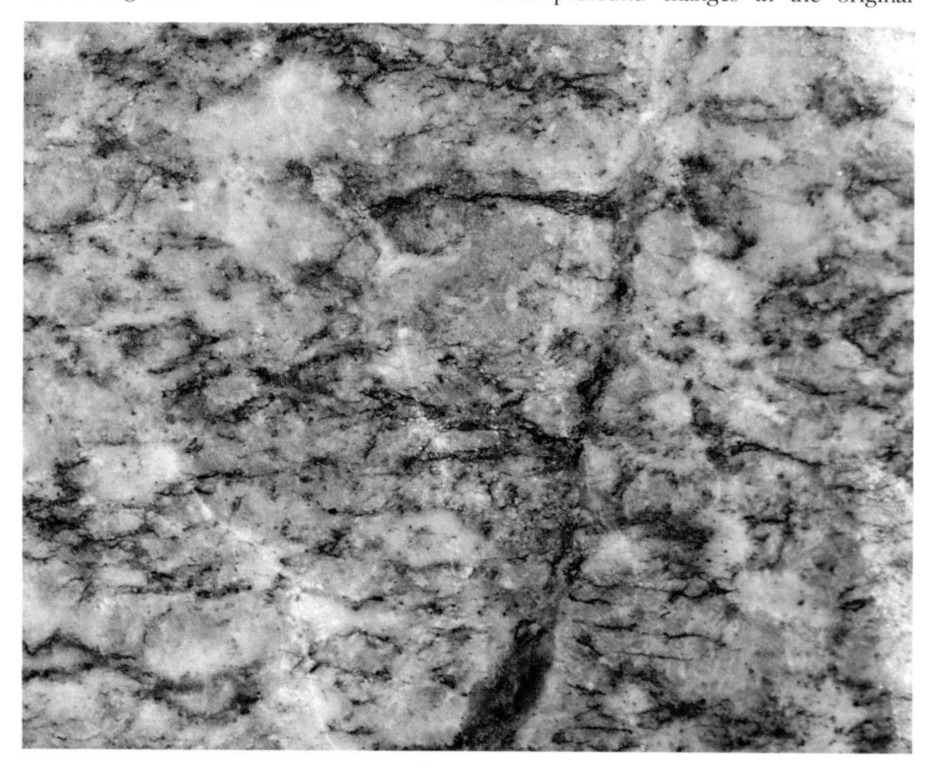

Marble

This rock develops when limestones are intruded by magma or overrun by lavas. The heat from the molten igneous rock brings about profound changes in the original limestone. Marbles are pale-coloured rocks, of medium to coarse grain size, but have a great variety of colours in the veins and streaks which run through them. These may be green, blue, red or black, depending on the minerals in them. Pale greens may, for example, be the result of the metamorphic mineral brucite. The main mineral in marble is calcite, and the other metamorphic minerals develop from impurities in the original rock. These may be (in addition to brucite) garnet, olivine, serpentine, tremolite and diopside.

Marble is different in texture and structure from the original limestone. Bedding and other sedimentary structures disappear because of the recrystallization which takes place. The original calcite in the limestone becomes an interlocking crystalline mass, and fossils made of calcite are also removed by the metamorphic processes. It may be difficult, however, to draw an exact boundary between marble and unmetamorphosed limestone at the outer limits of metamorphism, where metamorphic influences are weakest. Distinction between unchanged and the outer metamorphosed material may be equally blurred in the case of other rocks involved in thermal alteration.

Metaquartzite

To distinguish between this rock and quartzites developed from sedimentary processes the term metaquartzite is used. Metaquartzites develop from the contact metamorphism of arenaceous sediments such as sandstones and arkoses. They are pale-coloured rocks and may be confused with marbles on initial observation. There are many obvious differences, however. Marbles are softer than metaquartzites and react with dilute cold hydrochloric acid. When broken, they may also show the rhombic cleavage of the contained calcite crystals. Metaquartzite often shows a granoblastic texture, equal-sized crystals of quartz interlocking in a mosaic. These crystals are medium- to coarse-grained, and, because of the recrystallization which has taken place, bedding structures may be absent, though in some metaquartzites, where metamorphism has not been too strong, features such as cross bedding are visible. Other minerals in the matrix include feldspar and mica. Sandstones are often poorly cemented, and the grains can easily be rubbed off with the fingers. This is not so with metaquartzite, which is a crystalline rock, as the original quartz grains have increased in size and fused together.

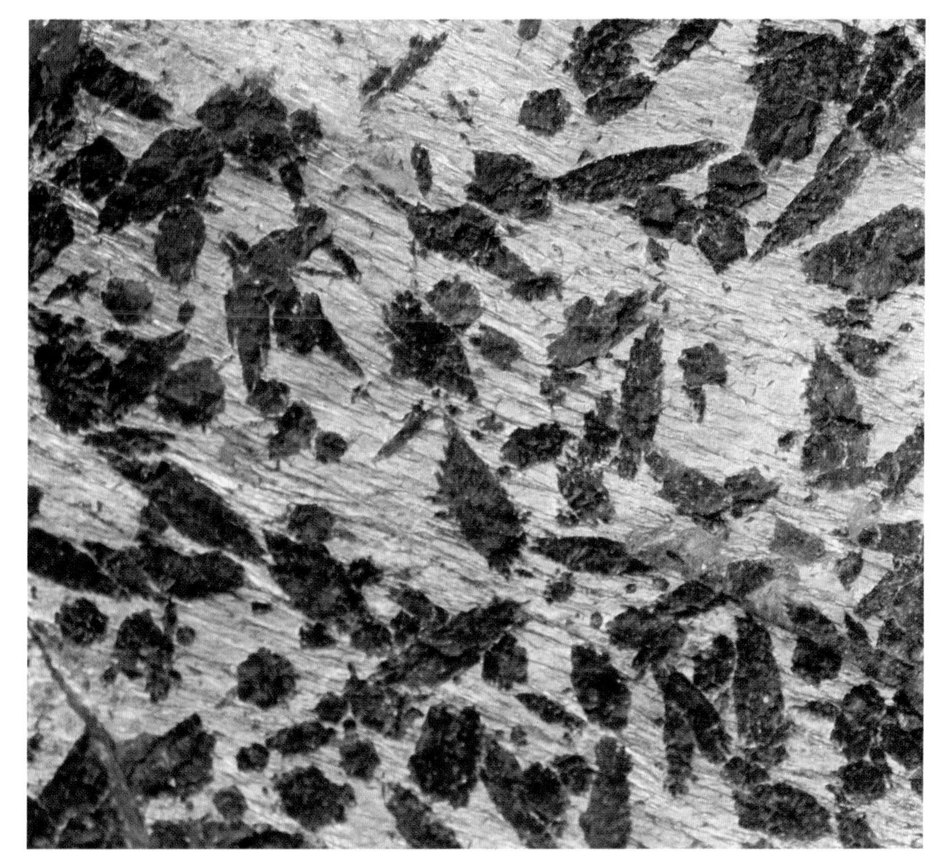

Above: *Hornfels. Formed near the margin of a granite batholith, this sample contains dark crystals of cordierite 5mm (1/5in) long. Hornfelses are very different from the sedimentary rocks prior to metamorphism.*

Hornfels

Hornfelses develop near the contact of hot, intrusive igneous rocks with pelitic sediments like shale and clay. They are among the most common of contact metamorphosed rocks. They exhibit a characteristic texture in which the mineral grains are of roughly the same size (equigranular) and are fused together in a mosaic, thereby suggesting that heat, rather than pressure, is the main metamorphic influence.

Hornfelses are tough, flinty rocks and contain minerals related to the parent material. Usually, hornfelses contain micas, quartz and feldspar, and a number of new metamorphic minerals form, depending on the proximity of the heat source. Nearest the magma sillimanite develops, with a zone of andalusite farther out and chiastolite at a yet greater distance. In the most distant area to be affected by the heat, hornfelses grade out into a zone of spotted rock. This is usually darkish-coloured with definite rounded masses of even darker material 1–3mm in diameter. These spots are often of chiastolite or cordierite.

Mylonite

This is a pulverized and welded rock formed along major thrust faults. When faulting takes place, rocks in the fault zone are fragmented and their component minerals and grains are streaked out in the direction of movement. They are usually fine-grained and compact rocks, with larger grains smoothed out and elongated and bound together by fine rock dust. This change in the original rock is called dynamic or cataclastic metamorphism.

Below: *Mylonite. Developed during large-scale thrust fault movement, this rock is characterised by streaked-out particles, well seen here. The pale, elongated fragments of quartz are 1cm (1/2in) long.*

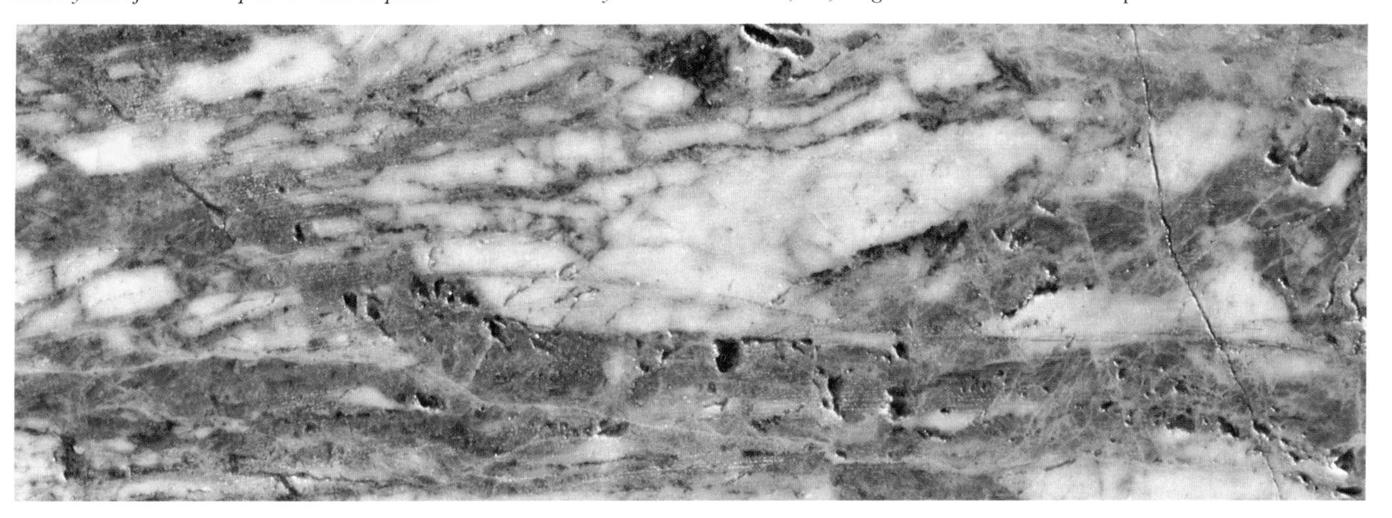

MINERALS

Some minerals are essential rock formers, while others occur as fine crystals in veins and fractures in the crustal rocks. Many are prized as gems; others, too, are of great economic significance, especially those which are ores of metals. Whatever their individual features, minerals are inorganic, occur naturally, and have chemical and physical properties which can be exactly defined.

In order to identify a given mineral specimen there are a number of tests and observations which can be made. The most striking feature of many minerals is their colour. This can vary from the bright yellow of orpiment to the rich blue of azurite and the purple of amethyst. The colour of a mineral is caused by the way light is absorbed or refracted within the crystalline structure and may indicate the presence of impurities. With many minerals colour is a very good guide for identification but it is not infallible, especially in the case of the more common varieties. Many of these, for example calcite, quartz, baryte, gypsum and halite, can be white in colour. Also, many minerals can exhibit a variety of colours: for example quartz, one of the commonest minerals, may be purple, green, yellow, brown, black, white or pink.

A property closely related to colour is streak. This is the colour of the powder of the mineral, and is more consistent than the sometimes variable colour of a hand specimen. The streak is obtained by drawing the mineral across the surface of an unglazed porcelain tile (a streak plate), or, in the case of very hard minerals, by scratching them with something tougher still. Many minerals have a white streak, including quartz in all its colour forms, but in some cases streak can be reasonably diagnostic, as with the red-brown streak of hematite.

The shapes which minerals form are a source of wonder, whether they are delicate crystals or a mass of bulbous forms. Crystals are understood by looking at their symmetry and are classified into six systems. Within a system there can be a variety of shapes as long as each fits the geometrical definition of that system. The diagram indicates some of this variety.

More important for identification than the system to which a mineral belongs is the shape of the specimen being examined. This is called the mineral habit, and can vary from a precise shape to an amorphous lump. Habit is described by a number of terms. Crystals may be prismatic (that is, of uniform cross-section), cubic, octahedral, and so on. Other habits may be fibrous, tabular (flat), acicular (needle-like), massive (of no definite shape), granular, botryoidal (like a bunch of grapes), reniform (kidney-shaped), stalactitic and mamillated (large and rounded).

Below: *The naturally formed crystals of minerals are classified according to their symmetry. There are six systems, from the cubic, with a high degree of symmetry, to the more complex hexagonal, which has less symmetry. An axis of symmetry is used to define each system (an imaginary line through the centre of a crystal, around which it can be rotated to give the same view at least twice). Within each of the symmetry groups, many different shapes and habits are possible, but all these can be referred to the same axis of symmetry as the model for a group.*

Minerals often break along a certain plane, determined by cleavage. This is related to the way in which the atoms making up a crystal are bound together. Cleavage faces are not as perfect as crystal faces but nevertheless reflect light consistently and are repeated many times over when a specimen is broken. Calcite, for example, breaks into rhombs, and mica cleaves into thin, flat plates. When a mineral breaks it does not always cleave. Indeed, some minerals like quartz never cleave, but fracture instead. This produces uneven, rough surfaces or curved conchoidal (shell-like) patterns which cannot be repeated precisely and which do not lie parallel as do many cleavage surfaces. By studying the way a mineral has broken it is possible to narrow down the identification still further.

Having looked at colour, shape and breakage, the mineral can now be tested for hardness. This gives a good indication of what the mineral may be, and the test can be

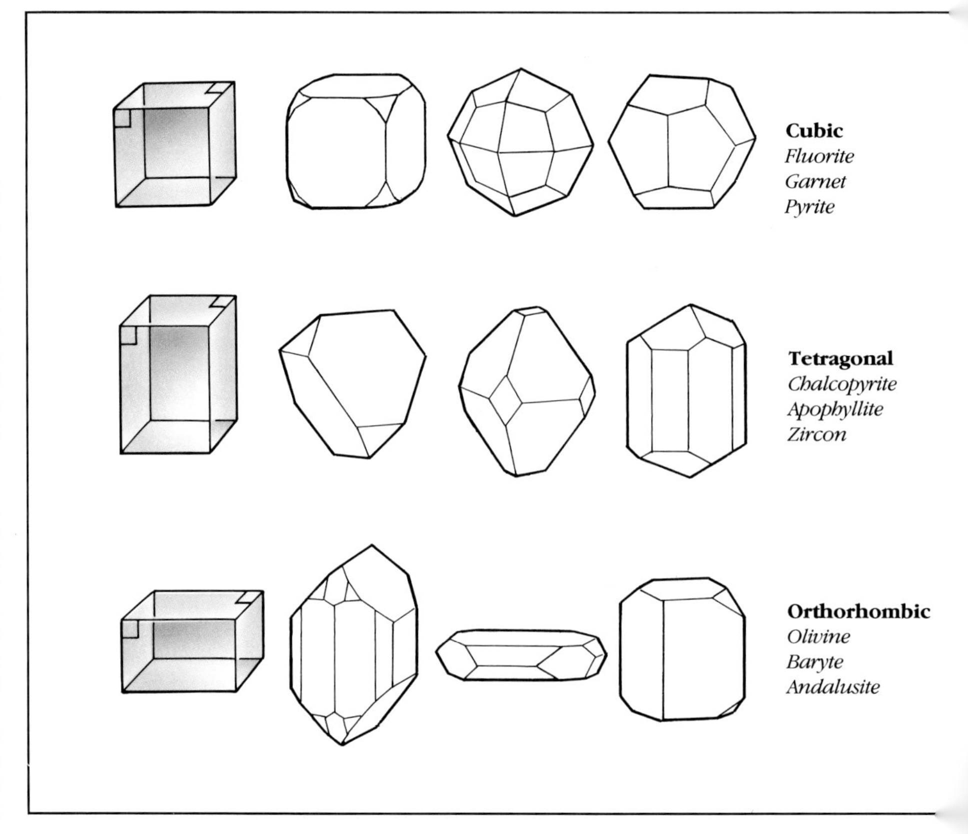

carried out with simple equipment. A fingernail, a coin and a penknife will usually be enough, though some mineral specimens of known hardness will also help. Hardness is measured against a scale first set up in 1812 by F. Mohs and still used today, probably because it employs common minerals to define its points. These, however, are not arranged at equal intervals. 1 is talc, 2 gypsum, 3 calcite, 4 fluorite, 5 apatite, 6 feldspar, 7 quartz, 8 topaz, 9 corundum and 10 diamond. A fingernail is 2½, a coin 3½ and a penknife 5½. The mineral being investigated is scratched by objects of known hardness in sequence from the softest upwards until the mineral is softer than the object. Care is needed to see what is actually scratching what.

A further property which can be measured very precisely is relative density. This is the actual weight of a mineral specimen compared with the weight of an equal volume of water. The density of water is taken as 1.0. However, the relative density often has to be estimated because special measuring equipment is needed for an accurate test. With practice it becomes easy to tell if a specimen has a higher than average density. Many common minerals like calcite and quartz have a relative density of about 2.6. Certain minerals can be easily identified by their density: baryte is 4.5 and galena 7.5.

A more subjective property which is used for identification is that called lustre. This is the way a mineral reflects the light falling upon it. There are a number of words used to describe certain lustres. These include vitreous (glassy), metallic, dull or earthy, silky, pearly, waxy and adamantine (brilliant).

When these properties have been investigated it should be possible from the 'identikit' picture which has been built up to find the mineral in a tabulated list of properties in one of the many reference books available. There are still other features which may help. Some minerals exhibit twinning, whereby two or more crystals share a certain crystallographic plane and grow together, often in an interlocking way. If the specimen being investigated shows this twinned habit, such as two cubes interlocking in the case of fluorite, identification may be further helped. Finally, some minerals exhibit special properties. Halite, for example, is salty to taste, and magnetite is magnetic at ordinary temperatures. Other minerals are readily soluble in weak acids, or may exhibit fluorescence or radioactivity.

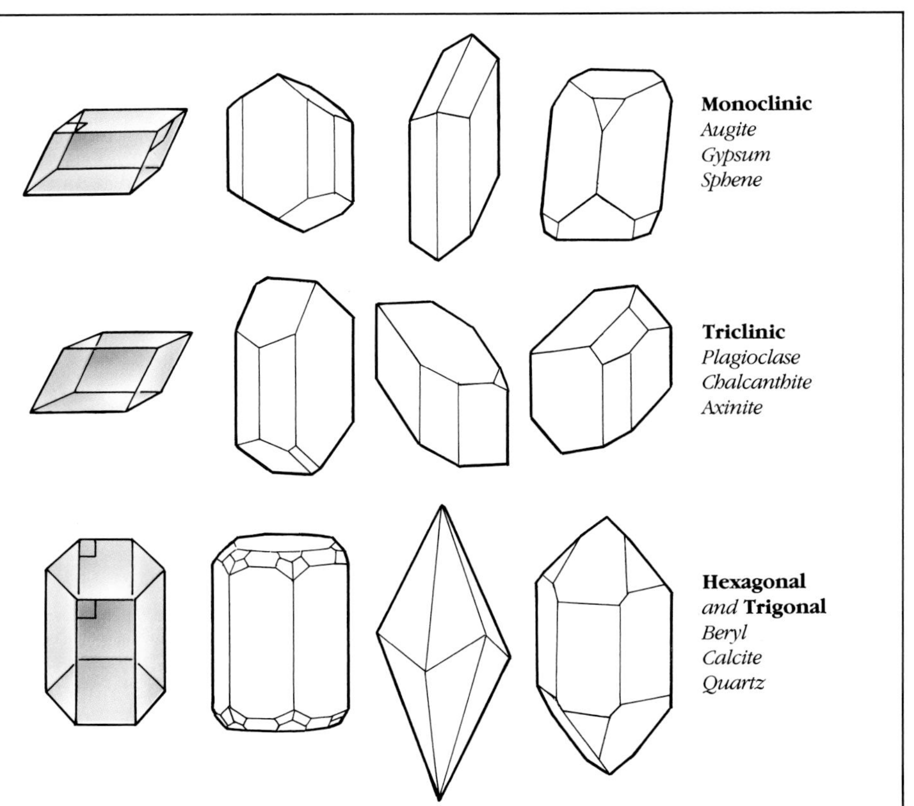

Monoclinic
Augite
Gypsum
Sphene

Triclinic
Plagioclase
Chalcanthite
Axinite

Hexagonal *and* **Trigonal**
Beryl
Calcite
Quartz

There are many ways in which minerals can form in the Earth. The rock-forming silicates like the feldspars, amphiboles, pyroxenes, micas and olivines form from magma or lava by direct crystallization. Other minerals are found naturally in sedimentary rocks; these include the evaporites, such as halite, gypsum and potash, precipitated from saline waters on the Earth's surface. Calcite and dolomite form the bulk of many limestones, and quartz can crystallize in the pore spaces in sandstones. The conditions of temperature and pressure which provoke metamorphic changes in preformed rocks also cause new minerals to form. Garnet, asbestos, talc and graphite are common among these, and under extreme conditions andalusite, cordierite and sillimanite may form.

Many of the most economically valuable and the most beautiful mineral specimens are found in mineral veins. Where fractures exist in the Earth's crust, solutions bearing the constituent particles for mineral formation flow upwards and precipitate their solids. These veins may extend for many kilometres and can be a number of metres wide. The origin of the mineralizing solutions, usually called hydrothermal fluids, may be the residual waters from magmatic consolidation or deeply trapped brines caught up in seabed sediments and then taken by movements within the Earth and burial under other strata to great depth. These solutions are very powerful chemically, being at many hundreds of degrees centigrade and under great pressure. From them a great variety of minerals may form. These include quartz, fluorite, baryte, calcite, dolomite, galena, sphalerite and many other metallic ore minerals.

Minerals also form from volcanic eruptions. Near to the vent of a volcano deposits of sulphur may occur, often with mercury and antimony minerals. Where volcanoes erupt beneath the sea very rich ore deposits are formed. These contain many metals such as manganese, copper, iron and zinc. Magma which solidifies deep underground can produce, through differentiation, large masses of metal ores, including those of platinum and chromium.

NATIVE ELEMENTS

Gold [Au]

This mineral crystallizes in the cubic system, though crystals are very rare, the usual habit being dendritic masses, nuggets or small grains. The colour is yellowish, but with an increase in the content of other metals such as silver it becomes paler. Gold breaks without cleavage and with a rough fracture. It is a very soft metal, being easily scratched with a knife blade and a coin; the hardness is 2½ to 3. Gold is malleable and has a yellowish streak and a metallic lustre. Its most obvious characteristic, apart from the colour, is its very high density, which ranges from 15.5 to 19.3 according to the degree of contamination with other metals. Gold does not tarnish and is insoluble in single acids. The specimen photographed shows a typical occurrence with quartz and is from a hydrothermal vein. Being a high-density mineral, gold is frequently found in placer deposits, occurring in sands and conglomerates.

Above: *Gold. In this sample, gold occurs in typical dendritic habit associated with white prismatic quartz crystals, formed in a hydrothermal vein. The specimen is from California (USA) and is 8cm (3¼in) across.*

Below: *Copper. This characteristic specimen has the brownish colour and some alteration to green malachite on the right-hand edge. The rough texture and dendritic habit are typical. The specimen is 6cm (2½in) across.*

Copper [Cu]

Copper forms crystals in the cubic system but, like gold, is usually found in dendritic shapes like the specimen shown here. When crystals occur they are usually cubes or rhombdodecahedra. The colour of native copper is reddish or brown, often with green patches of malachite on weathered parts. Copper does not cleave but fractures with a rough break. The hardness is between 2½ and 3, while the density is relatively high at 8.9. At best the lustre is metallic but copper is frequently weathered with a dull surface. This metal is malleable and is soluble in nitric acid. Copper is often found in the weathered regions of sulphide veins and also forms in basalts, where it can be a cavity filler. Sediments may contain copper as a replacement mineral.

Sulphur [S]

Native sulphur forms bright yellow tabular crystals which are classified in the orthorhombic system. It can also occur as massive specimens, and has a white streak and resinous lustre. There are no cleavage surfaces when sulphur breaks, merely an uneven fracture. It is a very soft mineral, having a hardness of only 1½ to 2½, and its density is also very low at 2.1. Sulphur is soluble in water and weak acids. A common occurrence is around vents and hot springs in volcanic areas.

Diamond [C]
Crystallizing in the cubic system, diamonds are usually in the form of rounded octahedral crystals. They can vary considerably in colour, from colourless to brown, yellow, green, grey and black. The streak, difficult to obtain because of diamond's hardness of 10, is white. Cleavage is octahedral and fracture conchoidal. The density is slightly above average at 3.5. The brilliant lustre of diamond is described as adamantine. Diamonds form in igneous rocks called kimberlites, which are of ultra-basic composition and occur at great depth in the crust in pipe-shaped masses. They are also found in sediments derived from these kimberlites.

Silver [Ag]
Silver normally forms in wiry masses, though it is classified in the cubic system. The bright silvery colour rapidly tarnishes to grey or brown. It has a rough fracture but no cleavage, and the hardness of this malleable metal is 2½ to 3, with a high density of 9.6 to 11. Silver has a metallic lustre and a silvery-white streak. It occurs among sulphides in hydrothermal veins and in placers with gold.

Above: *This rough diamond is only 7.5mm (¼in) long. It exhibits the rounded octahedral crystal habit and typical brilliant lustre.*

Below: *Sulphur. These bright yellow crystals are encrusting a lava fragment from Mount Etna, Sicily. The sample is 6cm (2½in) across.*

Bismuth [Bi]
Bismuth occurs in massive or dendritic aggregates, though rare crystals are in the hexagonal system. It has a pinkish-white colour which tarnishes to brown. The hardness is 2½ to 3½ and the density 9.8. Bismuth has a metallic lustre and basal cleavage. It is a brittle mineral with an uneven fracture, forming with other metals such as tin and silver in hydrothermal veins.

Graphite [C]
Graphite is chemically the same as diamond but forms rare crystals in the hexagonal system, usually occurring as massive or granular specimens. The colour and streak are black. Graphite has a greasy feel, with a hardness of only 1 to 2 and a density of 2.2. The lustre is sub-metallic or dull, and there is a perfect cleavage. This mineral commonly occurs in metamorphic rocks such as schists and slates and is occasionally found in pegmatites.

SULPHIDES

Chalcopyrite [$CuFeS_2$]

Chalcopyrite forms crystals in the tetragonal system but also occurs as massive or granular specimens. The colour is brass-yellow, with a greenish-black streak. It breaks with an uneven fracture and the cleavage is very poor. Chalcopyrite has a metallic lustre, a hardness of 3½ to 4 and a density of 4.1 to 4.3. It may be confused with iron pyrites but is much softer and yellower. This mineral is common in hydrothermal veins and is also found in porphyry copper deposits.

Bornite [Cu_5FeS_4]

Bornite occurs as cubic or octahedral crystals and as massive specimens. It has a coppery-red colour which readily tarnishes to brilliant iridescent purple. This variety is called peacock ore. There is no cleavage and an uneven fracture. Bornite has a black or grey streak and a metallic lustre. The hardness is 3 (it is easily scratched with a coin) and the density is between 4.9 and 5.4. Bornite is readily recognized by its iridescence. It forms in hydrothermal veins and as a result of magmatic segregation.

Below: *Chalcopyrite. This sample comes from Cumbria, in the UK, and measures 6cm (2½in) across. It has the characteristic yellowish colour and exhibits the common association of chalcopyrite with quartz, which shows up in the photograph as greyish crystals.*

Left: *Bornite. This specimen from Zambia, with the brilliant tarnished colouring typical of peacock ore, is 7.5cm (3in) across.*

Sphalerite [ZnS]

Sphalerite forms tetrahedral and rhombdodecahedral crystals in the cubic system. Sometimes the edges of the crystals are curved. It has a resinous or even adamantine lustre and is brownish to black in colour, occasionally with a yellowish tinge. Perfect cleavage surfaces are produced when sphalerite breaks and it has a conchoidal fracture. The hardness is between 3½ and 4 and the density 3.9 to 4.2. A common hydrothermal mineral, sphalerite often occurs with galena, fluorite and chalcopyrite.

Covellite, covelline [CuS]

Covellite or covelline often occurs as platy or tabular crystals in the hexagonal system, or as massive specimens. The colour is dark greyish-blue, often with iridescence. Covellite has a dark grey streak, perfect cleavage and an uneven fracture. The lustre is dull to metallic, and the hardness is very low at 1½ to 2. Density varies from 4.6 to 4.8. Covellite occurs in hydrothermal veins and also in the parts of copper deposits where secondary enrichment has occurred.

Enargite [$CuAsS_4$]

Enargite occurs in massive or lamellar form, or as crystals of tabular habit in the orthorhombic system. It has a black colour and streak and a metallic lustre. The cleavage is prismatic and the fracture uneven. Enargite has a hardness of 3 and a density of 4.4. It melts in a candle flame and occurs in hydrothermal veins with such minerals as pyrite, tetrahedrite, bornite and sphalerite.

Stannite [Cu_2SnFeS_4]

Stannite only very rarely forms crystals in the tetragonal system, more commonly occurring as massive or granular pieces. The lustre is metallic and the colour is bronze or steel-grey, with a black streak. It is a very brittle mineral which breaks with an uneven fracture. The hardness is 4 and the density 4.4. Stannite occurs in hydrothermal veins along with many other metallic minerals including cassiterite, galena, sphalerite and chalcopyrite.

Left: *Sphalerite. This sulphide of zinc is exploited for that metal. The sample here shows the brownish colour and is associated with pale calcite. It is 10cm (4in) across.*

Above: *Pyrite, or iron pyrites. This iron sulphide commonly forms good crystals. Here the left-hand one (1.5cm/⅝in across) has a typical cubic habit, and the other is a pyritohedron. Both show twinning, with smaller crystals growing from them.*

Pyrite, iron pyrites [FeS_2]

Pyrite forms perfect cubes and octahedra in the cubic system, as in the specimen shown here. It can also occur as nodules and as massive specimens. Striations often cover the faces of the cubes. It is a pale yellowish colour, not as deep yellow as copper pyrite (chalcopyrite). The streak is greenish black and the lustre metallic. Pyrite is brittle, with indistinct cleavage and an uneven or conchoidal fracture. The hardness is high at 6 to 6½ and the density is 4.8 to 5.2. Pyrite is a common mineral which forms in many ways. It is found in association with other sulphides in hydrothermal veins and as an accessory mineral in some igneous rocks, especially granites. Perfect crystals occur in slates, and pyrite often replaces organic material in fossils. Some shale strata contain rows of pyrite nodules.

Galena [PbS]

Galena very often forms perfect cubes and octahedra in the cubic system. It is metallic lead-grey in colour, though when freshly broken it may be bright blue. The streak is a characteristic lead-grey. When broken the

Below: *Galena. Here the silvery-grey crystals of this lead sulphide are associated with a mass of white quartz. Both minerals commonly occur together in hydrothermal veins. Some of the galena crystals show the cubic cleavage. The specimen is 7.5cm (3in) across.*

Right: *Cinnabar. The bright red granular masses of this sulphide of mercury are shown encrusting a fragment of volcanic rock. Cinnabar often forms around volcanoes. The sample, from Spain, is 10cm (4in) across.*

mineral cleaves into perfect cubes, whereas the fracture may be uneven or conchoidal. The hardness is only 2½ but the density is very high at 7.5. Galena is easily identified by its colour, habit and density. It occurs in hydrothermal veins with other sulphides such as quartz, calcite, fluorite and baryte. A chemical test which may be carried out is to add some galena to warm hydrochloric acid. Hydrogen sulphide gas, with its characteristic smell of bad eggs, is produced.

Cinnabar [HgS]

Cinnabar forms as rhombohedral and tabular crystals in the hexagonal system, as well as in granular and massive form. The colour is very characteristic, being rich red or red-brown, with a bright red streak. The lustre varies from dull to metallic or adamantine. When broken, cinnabar has a prismatic cleavage or an uneven fracture. The hardness is 2 to 2½, while the density is 8.1. This mineral forms with realgar and pyrite near hot springs and volcanic craters. In sediments of placer type cinnabar results from the weathering and erosion of mercury-bearing rocks.

Orpiment [As_2S_3]

As in the specimen shown here, orpiment commonly forms massive pieces, though it crystallizes in the monoclinic system. The characteristic colour is bright yellow, but it can be orange or brown. The streak is yellow and the lustre is dull, resinous or pearly. It is a very soft mineral, having a hardness of 1½ to 2, and the density is 3.5. When broken it cleaves to produce thin, flexible plates. Orpiment forms in mineral veins and around hot springs.

Below: *Orpiment is a sulphide of arsenic. If handled, poisonous yellow powder sticks to the fingers. This sample is 9cm (3½in) across.*

Marcasite [FeS_2]

Marcasite forms prismatic crystals in the orthorhombic system as well as nodular and radiating masses. It has a pale bronze colour, a metallic lustre and an almost black streak. When it is broken, the cleavage is indistinct and prismatic and the fracture is uneven. Marcasite has a hardness of 6 to 6½ and a density of 4.9. It is paler than pyrite and also slightly less dense. It forms in hydrothermal veins but at lower temperatures than pyrite. In some sedimentary rocks, such as chalk, marcasite occurs as discrete nodular masses which have a radiating internal structure.

Realgar [AsS]

Realgar is a bright red mineral which forms prismatic crystals in the monoclinic system and also occurs in granular or massive form. The streak is orange or red, and the lustre is resinous. There is a good cleavage with conchoidal or uneven fracture. The hardness is 1½ to 2 and the density is 3.6. Realgar is formed in hydrothermal veins and around hot springs, and is often associated with orpiment, tin, lead and silver.

Above: *Arsenopyrite. This characteristic specimen from Portugal shows the monoclinic crystals, silvery-grey colour and bright metallic lustre. It is 8.5cm (3½in) across.*

Below: *Stibnite. This sulphide of antimony often has thin needle-like crystals. Here the grey metallic stibnite is set in white quartz. The sample is 8cm (3¼in) across.*

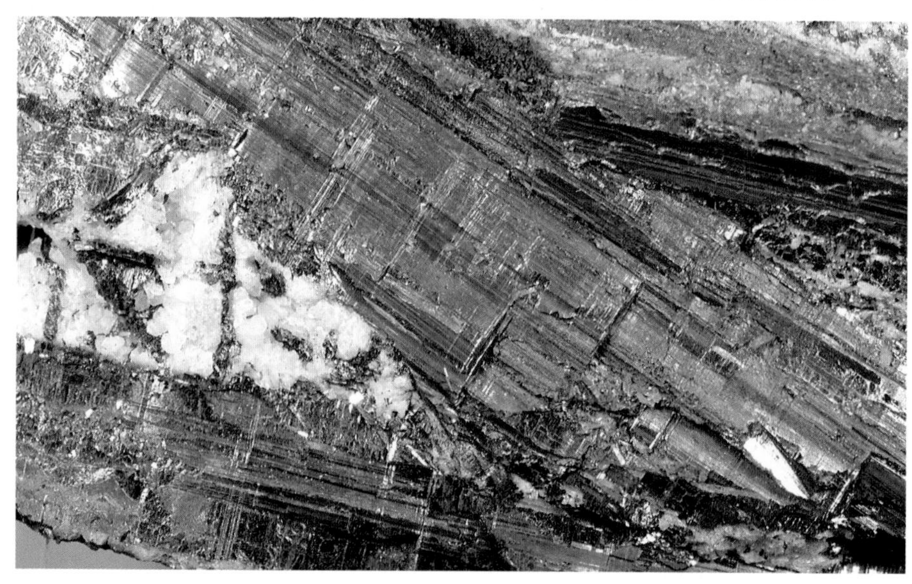

Arsenopyrite [FeAsS]

Arsenopyrite forms prismatic crystals in the monoclinic system and also occurs as granular and massive pieces. It is a silvery-coloured mineral with a metallic lustre and tarnishes to a brownish colour. The streak is black. When broken it fractures unevenly or cleaves prismatically. The hardness of arsenopyrite is 5½ to 6 and the density is high at 5.9 to 6.2. This mineral is found in hydrothermal veins, often with silver, tin and gold. It occasionally occurs in pegmatites.

Stibnite [Sb_2S_3]

Stibnite occurs as prismatic or needle-like crystals (acicular habit) which, as can be seen in the specimen shown, have lengthwise striations. It also occurs in granular or massive form. When tarnished the lustre is dull, but when fresh, stibnite has a metallic lustre with a grey colour and streak. This is a brittle mineral which fractures conchoidally and cleaves lengthwise. It is soft at hardness 2 and has a density of 4.5 to 4.6. Stibnite melts in a match flame. Found in hydrothermal veins, it is often associated with quartz and also occurs around hot springs.

Molybdenite [MoS_2]

Molybdenite commonly occurs as flat platy masses but it can be granular. The plates may have a hexagonal outline and the mineral is classified in the hexagonal system. The specimen shown here exhibits a radiating habit. It has a metallic lustre and the colour is bluish-grey or lead-grey with a grey streak. Molybdenite has a greasy feel and cleaves into flexible plates. The hardness is only 1 to 1½, and the density 4.6 to 4.8. The example here shows a typical occurrence on granite, and it also occurs in veins, though never in large masses.

Tetrahedrite [$(Cu,Fe)_{12}(Sb,As)_4S_{13}$]

Tetrahedrite is one of a series called the tetrahedrite-tennantite series. Both minerals are very similar in their structure and properties. The crystal system is cubic and the habit varies from massive and granular to tetrahedral crystals. Tetrahedrite is grey, with a metallic lustre, while tennantite is bluish-grey. The streak is black. When broken there is no cleavage but a conchoidal or uneven fracture. The hardness is quite low at 3 to 4½, and the density is 4.6 to 5.2. These minerals occur in hydrothermal veins, often with zinc, copper and lead ores.

Bournonite [$PbCuSbS_3$]

Bournonite is often called 'wheel ore' because the crystals are commonly like cog wheels. It also forms with granular and tabular habit. This mineral has a metallic lustre, a black or dark colour and a black streak. The fracture is uneven and the cleavage is very poor. It is a very soft mineral at 2½ to 3, and the density is 5.9. This is another hydrothermal vein mineral, being found with other metallic sulphides.

Cobaltite [CoAsS]

Cobaltite forms as cubic crystals or as granular and massive specimens. It has a metallic lustre and a silvery-grey colour, with a dark grey streak. The broken mineral will show a cubic cleavage and an uneven fracture. The hardness is 5½ and the density 6.3, both these features being useful for identification. Cobaltite forms with other metallic minerals in hydrothermal veins.

Below: *Molybdenite. The silvery-grey crystals of this molybdenum sulphide stand out from the pinkish feldspar of granite. The specimen, from Cumbria, UK, is 10cm (4in) across.*

HALIDES

Halite [NaCl]

Halite is also sometimes called rock salt. It forms cubic crystals which often have hollowed faces (hopper crystals) and can be granular or massive, with typical smoothed surfaces which result from halite's solubility. This mineral has a vitreous lustre when freshly broken or on a perfect crystal face but soon becomes greasy. Halite can exhibit a variety of colours. Commonly it is white or pale orange but it can be colourless, black, blue, yellow and grey. The streak is white.

Below: *The pale orange colour is typical of halite, which is formed from sodium chloride and has a salty taste. Its extreme solubility is shown by the rounded edges of this specimen, measuring 12cm (4¾in) across.*

When broken a perfect cubic cleavage occurs and the fracture is uneven. It is a soft mineral at 2½ and the density is very low at 2.2. Halite has a distinct salty taste and is very soluble in cold water. It forms as an evaporite by precipitation when saline water dries up, and is associated with gypsum, sylvine and dolomite rock, often interbedded with marls.

Sylvine, sylvite [KCl]

This mineral commonly occurs as massive specimens, or as octahedra and cubes within the cubic system. With a vitreous lustre, sylvine has a red, white or grey colour and a white streak. The fracture is uneven and the cleavage cubic. It is very soft at hardness 2 (less than halite), and the density is only 2.0. The taste is more bitter than that of halite, and it is more soluble in water. Sylvine is found in evaporite deposits with halite.

SULPHATES

Fluorite, fluorspar [CaF_2]

Fluorite often occurs as perfect cubes, many of which interlock with each other. Octahedral and rhombdodecahedral crystals are not uncommon. Banded fluorite and nodular masses also occur. 'Blue John', which is found in Derbyshire, England, is a banded variety. This mineral shows considerable variation in colour, ranging from the green of the specimen in the photograph to blue and purple, black and yellowish. The streak is white and the lustre vitreous. The cleavage causes the corners of the cubes to become broken off, leaving triangular surfaces (octahedral cleavage). It has a conchoidal or uneven fracture. Fluorite is the definition of 4 on the hardness scale, so it is harder than a coin, and it has a density of 3.3. This mineral is extremely common in hydrothermal veins and is found in association with the metallic sulphides as well as with quartz, calcite and baryte. It may also be found as an accessory in granite.

Gypsum [$CaSO_4.2H_20$]

Gypsum forms a variety of habits and crystallizes in the monoclinic system. The specimen shown here is of the 'desert rose' variety, while other habits are 'satin spar', with thin prismatic fibrous crystals, and 'daisy gypsum', with radiating structures. Selenite is the name given to the monoclinic form with transparent crystals. The lustre is pearly or vitreous, and the colour varies from white to pink, brown or grey. The streak is white. When broken, gypsum fractures unevenly but it cleaves perfectly. Gypsum defines hardness 2 on the scale, so it can easily be scratched with a fingernail. Its density is very low at 2.2. It forms in evaporite deposits with halite and sylvine, and also crystallizes in the form of selenite in clay strata and around hot springs.

Baryte, barite, barytes [$BaSO_4$]

Baryte occurs in a variety of habits from tabular and prismatic crystals to fibrous and cockscomb (like a cockerel's crest, as photographed here). It also has a great variety of colours, ranging from white to brown, red, green and blue, and a vitreous lustre. The streak is white. It breaks with a perfect cleavage and an uneven or conchoidal fracture. Baryte is not hard at 2½ to 3½, but is noticeably heavy at a density of 4.5. It forms in hydrothermal veins.

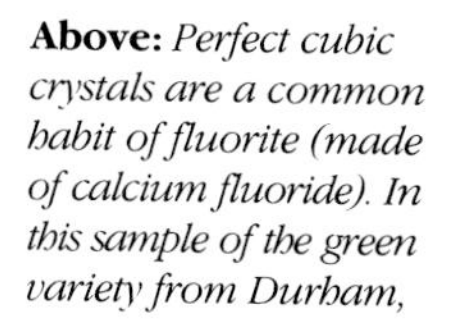

Above: *Perfect cubic crystals are a common habit of fluorite (made of calcium fluoride). In this sample of the green variety from Durham, UK, many of the cubes show twinning and are a maximum of 1cm (3/8in) across. Fluorite is used as a flux in the steel-making industry.*

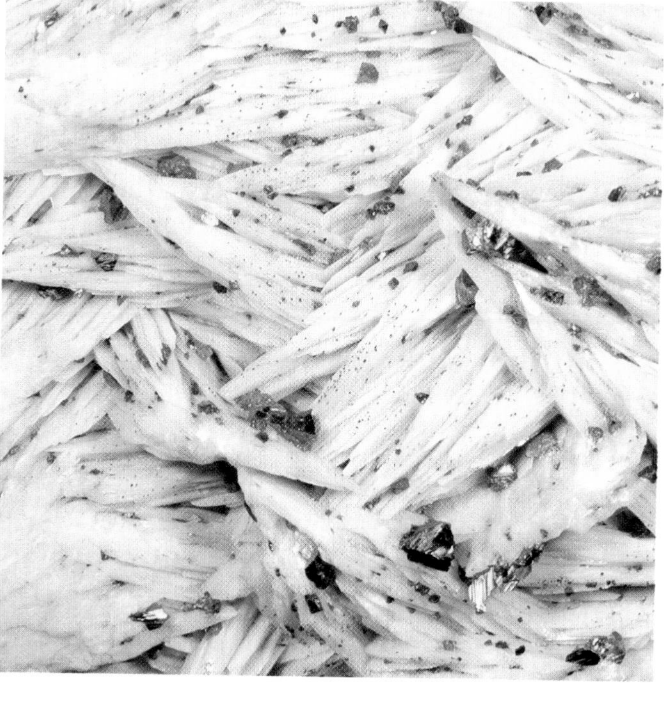

Above: *Baryte is made of barium sulphate, is often pale in colour and has an unusually high density. This specimen, from Dreislar, Germany, shows a cockscomb habit and has small crystals of yellowish chalcopyrite among the baryte crystals. It is 8.5cm (3 3/8in) across.*

Below: *Gypsum. This evaporite mineral has a number of habits, the one seen here in close-up being the desert rose variety. Made of hydrated calcium sulphate, gypsum is used for making plaster. The photograph covers left to right 11.5cm (4 1/2in) of a sizeable specimen.*

CARBONATES

Calcite [$CaCO_3$]

Calcite often forms beautiful prismatic crystals, as in the specimen photographed. These can be either pointed (dog-tooth) or have flat tops (nail-head). The crystals are in the hexagonal system, and the habit of calcite is more varied than that of any other mineral. It can be massive, granular, fibrous or stalactitic. Joined (twinned) crystals are very common. The lustre is vitreous or pearly, and the colour varies from white or colourless and transparent to yellow, green and brown. The streak is white. When broken, calcite cleaves into perfect rhombs with parallelogram faces. Transparent cleavage rhombs show double refraction and are called Iceland Spar. The fracture is uneven or conchoidal. Calcite is the definition of 3 on the hardness scale, and its density is 2.7. When cold dilute hydrochloric acid is poured on to a fragment of calcite, a vigorous effervescence occurs and carbon dioxide gas is produced. This mineral forms in hydrothermal veins, limestones and marbles, in evaporite deposits and around hot springs.

Above: *Calcite. This common form of calcium carbonate is seen here as fine hexagonal crystals. There is much twinning, and the prismatic crystals have a flat-topped, nail-head habit. The specimen is from Egremont in Cumbria, UK, well known for fine specimens, and is 15cm (6in) across.*

Below: *Rhodochrosite. The banded structure of this manganese carbonate mineral is most attractive when cut and polished. This sample, from Argentina, is 10cm (4in) across.*

Rhodochrosite [$MnCO_3$]

Rhodochrosite usually occurs as massive banded specimens, as in the photograph, or in granular or reniform masses. The rhombohedral crystals, belonging to the hexagonal system, often have curved faces. With a vitreous lustre, this mineral is typically pink to deep reddish pink in colour but can also be grey or light brown. The streak is white. When broken there is a rhombohedral cleavage or an uneven fracture. The hardness of rhodochrosite is 3½ to 4½, and the density is 3.3 to 3.7. This is another mineral which effervesces with cold dilute hydrochloric acid, but its colour, habit and hardness distinguish it from calcite. It forms in hydrothermal veins and in some metamorphosed sedimentary rocks.

Cerussite [$PbCO_3$]

This mineral forms thin prismatic crystals in the orthorhombic system which typically make a radiating mass (see the photograph on page 3). The lustre is adamantine, and the colour varies from white to grey or brownish. There is a white streak. It is a brittle mineral with a prismatic cleavage and a conchoidal fracture, and has a hardness of 3 to 3½. Because of the lead in its chemical structure, cerussite has a high density of 6.5. It is found in lead deposits, especially where they have been altered by oxidation.

Above: *The hydrated copper carbonates malachite (green) and azurite (blue) often occur together in the altered parts of copper deposits. This specimen is 6.5cm (2½in) across.*

Malachite [$Cu_2CO_3(OH)_2$]

Malachite generally occurs as banded and botryoidal specimens but can also be granular. Crystals are rare and form in the monoclinic system as thin needles. It has a silky lustre on the broken parts of the banded masses, and it is well known for its bright green colour. The streak is green, and the mineral breaks with a good cleavage or a subconchoidal to uneven fracture. Malachite reacts with cold dilute hydrochloric acid. It has a hardness of 3½ to 4 and a density of 4.0. It is a not uncommon mineral associated with copper veins and is formed by the oxidation of minerals in these veins.

Azurite [$Cu_3(CO_3)_2(OH)_2$]

Azurite is usually in massive form but can also occur as radiating prismatic groups of crystals in the monoclinic system. The dark blue colour and streak are very characteristic, and there is a vitreous lustre. The broken mineral shows a prismatic cleavage and a conchoidal fracture; it is brittle. The hardness is 3½ to 4, and the density is 3.8. Azurite often occurs with malachite, as on the specimen shown here, forming in the oxidised parts of copper veins.

Above: *Dolomite. Here, brownish rhombs of dolomite with typical curved faces are associated with two forms of hematite – red-brown kidney ore and black specularite. The sample, is 20cm (8in) across.*

Below: *Aragonite is a harder form of calcium carbonate than calcite and here forms delicate acicular crystals. It is not as common as calcite and lacks calcite's rhombic cleavage. The specimen is 8.5cm (3¼in) across.*

Siderite [$FeCO_3$]

Siderite forms rhombohedral crystals which typically have curved faces. It can also form with granular or massive habit, and the crystal system is hexagonal. When broken, this mineral shows a rhombohedral cleavage and an uneven fracture. The colour is usually a greyish-brown but it can also be black. The streak is white. Siderite has a dull or vitreous lustre and a hardness of 3½ to 4½. The density is between 3.7 and 4.0. This is another of the many minerals which form in hydrothermal veins and it can also occur in beds of shale and clay as rounded nodules and concretions.

Witherite [$BaCO_3$]

This mineral forms massive or botryoidal specimens as well as prismatic crystals in the orthorhombic system. It is vitreous, with a white or yellowish colour and a white streak. The fracture is uneven and the cleavage good. The hardness is 3½, and because of the barium in its chemical structure it has a high density at 4.3. Witherite forms in hydrothermal veins along with baryte and galena.

Dolomite [$CaMg(CO_3)_2$]

Dolomite often forms rhombohedral crystals in the hexagonal system which have curved faces. This can be well seen in the specimen photographed. It can also occur in massive or granular form. The colour is typically pale brown, but can also be white, with a white streak. The lustre may be either vitreous or pearly. When broken, dolomite shows a rhombohedral cleavage and a conchoidal fracture. The hardness is 3½ to 4, with a density of 2.8 to 2.9. Dolomite forms as a hydrothermal mineral and in many limestones.

Aragonite [$CaCO_3$]

As in the specimen shown here, aragonite can form acicular (needle-like) crystals. It can also occur as pseudo-hexagonal twinned crystals and prisms in the orthorhombic system and as coral-like masses. It has a vitreous lustre, and a colour varying from white to pink, green, blue and red. The streak is white. When broken, aragonite fractures conchoidally and cleaves only indistinctly. It has a hardness of 3½ to 4, greater than chemically similar calcite, and the density is 2.9. Aragonite reacts with dilute hydrochloric acid but is harder than calcite and lacks the rhombic cleavage. It forms around hot springs and as an evaporite, and is sometimes found in glaucophane schists and oxidised metal deposits.

Smithsonite [$ZnCO_3$]

This mineral often forms reniform masses, as in the specimen shown here. Occasionally it occurs as rhombohedral crystals in the hexagonal system. It has a vitreous lustre, and the colour varies from green to grey, blue, brown or white. When broken, the fracture is uneven and the cleavage rhombohedral. It has a hardness of 5½, and the density is 4.3 to 4.5. Smithsonite forms in hydrothermal veins and in the weathered parts of zinc veins.

Above: *Smithsonite is composed of zinc carbonate. The colour varies, but this specimen of the quite common green variety shows the typical rounded reniform habit. It is from Ireland and is 14cm (5½in) across.*

Magnesite [$MgCO_3$]

Magnesite occurs only rarely as prismatic or rhombohedral crystals in the hexagonal system. Usually it is in fibrous, massive or granular form. It has a subvitreous lustre and is often coloured white, but impurities such as iron give it a brown or yellow colour. The streak is white. It has a hardness varying from 3½ to 4½ and a density of 3.0. When broken, the fracture is uneven or conchoidal and the cleavage rhombohedral. Magnesite reacts with dilute hydrochloric acid but only when warmed. This mineral forms when serpentinites and ultra-basic rocks are altered by the action of fluids rich in carbonic acid. It may also replace calcite and dolomite in limestones and form in hydrothermal veins.

OXIDES

Corundum [Al_2O_3]

Corundum belongs to the hexagonal crystal system. It forms as characteristically barrel-shaped crystals, but can also be massive and granular. There are a number of colour varieties of corundum, some of which are gem stones. The bright red variety illustrated in both cut and uncut forms is ruby, while blue corundum is sapphire. It can also be colourless, yellowish and grey. The streak of this very hard mineral, the definition of point 9 on the scale, is difficult to obtain but is white. Corundum has no cleavage and fractures unevenly or conchoidally. It has a very bright lustre varying from vitreous to adamantine. This feature enhances its gem-stone qualities of colour and great hardness. The density is slightly above average at 3.9 to 4.1. Corundum forms in igneous rocks, especially syenite, and in metamorphic rocks such as schist, gneiss and marble. It often accumulates in river sediments derived from a primary source by weathering.

Above: *Corundum, one of the hardest minerals. The red variety – ruby – is a precious gem-stone, shown here in its rough form in a schist matrix (15cm/6in long) as well as cut and faceted.*

Below: *Grains of spinel (magnesium aluminium oxide) produced by weathering and erosion of a primary source. The grains, from river sands in Sri Lanka, are 5mm (1/5in) across.*

Spinel [$MgAl_2O_4$]

Spinel forms as octahedral crystals in the cubic system but also commonly occurs in massive form. This mineral can exhibit a great variety of colours, ranging from red and pink (see photograph) to black, grey, green, blue, brown and white. The streak is greyish but difficult to obtain because of the great hardness of 8. The lustre is vitreous and the fracture conchoidal, there being no cleavage. Spinel has a density of 3.5 to 4.1. The great variation in the colour of this mineral is the result of slight changes in the chemistry, iron, zinc, chromium and manganese substituting for magnesium. Hercynite is a black variety containing iron, pleonaste is dark green and contains iron, gahnite contains zinc and is dark green, and picotite is brown, containing iron and chromium. Spinel forms in some basic and ultra-basic igneous rocks and in limestones which have been heated by contact metamorphism. It also accumulates in placer deposits.

Hematite [Fe_2O_3]

Hematite usually forms as massive or reniform specimens (the latter being known as kidney ore), but can form tabular or rhombohedral crystals in the hexagonal system. The streak is one of its most characteristic features, being a rusty red-brown colour. The colour is also usually reddish, but can be steel-grey or black. Specularite is a black crystalline form. There is no cleavage and an uneven fracture. The lustre varies from metallic to dull. Hematite has a high density at 4.9 to 5.3, and the hardness is also high at 5½ to 6½. It occurs as a hydrothermal mineral and as a replacement mineral, sometimes in huge deposits, and can also form as an accessory in some igneous rocks. Hematite is shown with dolomite on page 42.

Magnetite [Fe_3O_4]

Magnetite commonly forms as granular specimens but may occur as octahedral crystals in the cubic system. It is a black mineral with a black streak. The lustre may vary from dull to metallic. When it is broken there is no cleavage and an uneven to conchoidal fracture. This is a hard mineral at 5½ to 6½, and its density is 5.2. Magnetite, as the name suggests, is strongly magnetic at ordinary temperatures. A specimen of magnetite deflects a compass needle and attracts iron filings. This mineral is found in basic and ultra-basic rocks, and deposits of great economic significance can form through magmatic segregation. When weathered from its primary source, magnetite accumulates as a placer deposit, colouring alluvial sands black.

Below: *Magnetite. This black form of iron oxide is a very rich ore of iron and is therefore of importance to industry. The sample here is from Nordmark, Sweden, a well-known source. Being magnetic at ordinary temperatures, magnetite attracts iron filings. The specimen is 16cm (6½in) across.*

Above: *Cassiterite. This specimen is from Cornwall, UK, once a major world producer of tin. It is 8cm (3¼in) across.*

Below: *Bauxite forms through the alteration of aluminium silicates in tropical climates. This west African specimen is 20cm (8in) across.*

Cassiterite [SnO_2]

Cassiterite usually forms prismatic pyramidal crystals in the tetragonal system. It may also be massive and granular. It is a dark-coloured oxide mineral, being black or deep brownish, but the streak is white or grey. The lustre is usually metallic but can also be adamantine. When broken, cassiterite shows a prismatic cleavage and an uneven fracture. Both the hardness and density are very high, at 6 to 7 and 6.8 and 7.2 respectively. This mineral, which is an important ore of tin, forms in hydrothermal veins, especially near to granite batholiths.

Bauxite [$Al_2O_3.2H_2O$ plus iron oxides]

This mineral is an aggregate of several aluminium and iron oxides. The habit of bauxite is as massive or rounded specimens which have a reddish-brown or brownish-yellow colour. It is impossible to describe bauxite in the same terms as other minerals, mainly because of its very varied chemistry. It forms as a result of the weathering, especially in tropical climates, of a variety of rocks which contain aluminium silicates.

Pyrolusite [MnO_2]

Pyrolusite commonly forms non-crystalline masses with a reniform, dendritic or fibrous habit. It can crystallize in the tetragonal system and is a black metallic oxide with a black streak. When broken, this very brittle mineral has an uneven fracture or a prismatic cleavage. The hardness is very variable, rare crystals measuring 6 to 6½, but massive or fibrous specimens scoring only 1 to 2. The density is between 4.7 and 5.1. Pyrolusite forms in nodules on the ocean floor and as a precipitate in lakes and bogs.

Below: *The dendritic, or plant-like, habit characteristic of pyrolusite, an oxide of manganese. It also forms as massive specimens, which can be identified by their dull appearance and softness. This sample, from Germany, is 6cm (2½in) across.*

Chromite [$FeCr_2O_4$]

Chromite can form octahedral crystals in the cubic system but more usually occurs in granular or massive habit. With a metallic lustre, this oxide is dark brown or black in colour and has a brown streak. The hardness is quite high at 5½ and the density varies from 4.5 to 4.8. There is no cleavage but when broken the uneven fracture is apparent. Chromite occurs initially in ultra-basic igneous rocks, sometimes in discrete layers, and is also found in placer deposits.

Rutile [TiO_2]

Rutile usually forms as prismatic or pyramidal crystals in the tetragonal system, though it can also be massive. The thin acicular crystals of this oxide often occur embedded in quartz. It has a bright adamantine or metallic lustre and is variable in colour from black to yellow. The streak is brown. When broken, rutile has an uneven fracture or a prismatic cleavage. It is a hard mineral at 6 to 6½ and has a density of 4.3. Apart from its formation in quartz, this mineral occurs in high-grade metamorphic rocks like gneiss and schist and also in granites as an accessory mineral.

Cuprite [Cu_2O]

Cuprite occurs as cubic or octahedral crystals in the cubic system, or in granular and massive form. It is an oxide and is coloured black or reddish, with a red-brown streak and a metallic lustre. The hardness is from 3½ to 4 and the density 5.8 to 6.2. Cuprite has no cleavage and an uneven fracture. This mineral forms in copper veins where weathering has altered the primary copper minerals.

HYDROXIDES

Psilomelane $[BaMn^{2+}Mn^{4+}{}_8O_{16}(OH)_4]$

Psilomelane forms as stalactitic, massive or reniform specimens and crystallizes occasionally in the monoclinic system. It is black in colour with a black streak and a metallic or dull lustre. When broken there is an uneven fracture and no cleavage. It is hard but variable at 5 to 7, and the density is 3.5 to 4.7. Psilomelane forms in the altered parts of manganese veins and it is sometimes encountered in veins of quartz.

Manganite [MnO(OH)]

Manganite is a mineral which commonly forms as bundles of radiating prismatic crystals classified in the monoclinic system. With a sub-metallic lustre, it is dark grey to black in colour and has a black or red-brown streak. Manganite breaks to produce a prismatic cleavage and an uneven fracture. It is fairly soft at 4 on the hardness scale, and the density is 4.2 to 4.4. This mineral forms in hydrothermal veins and mineral deposits which have been weathered and oxidised, often with pyrolusite.

Above: *Psilomelane, a hydrated oxide of barium and manganese, often forms reniform masses. This specimen (15cm/6in across) has the characteristic metallic lustre.*

Left: *Goethite, a hydrated oxide of iron, typically forms in the stalactitic or botryoidal habit in the altered parts of iron deposits. This specimen is 10cm (4in) across.*

Goethite and limonite [FeO(OH)]

These two minerals have a similar chemistry although their properties and general appearance are very different. Goethite often forms botryoidal or stalactitic masses as shown in the photograph, although it can also occur as prismatic crystals in the orthorhombic system. The colour is black or very dark brown, with a metallic lustre, and the streak is brownish-yellow. Goethite feels greasy to the touch. When broken, it exhibits an uneven fracture but also cleaves perfectly in one direction. It is a hard mineral at 5 to 5½ and has a density of 3.4 to 4.3.

Limonite has quite different properties. It is bright yellow in colour and when tested for hardness or streak, it readily disintegrates into a yellow-brown powder. It has a dull or earthy lustre and an amorphous habit,

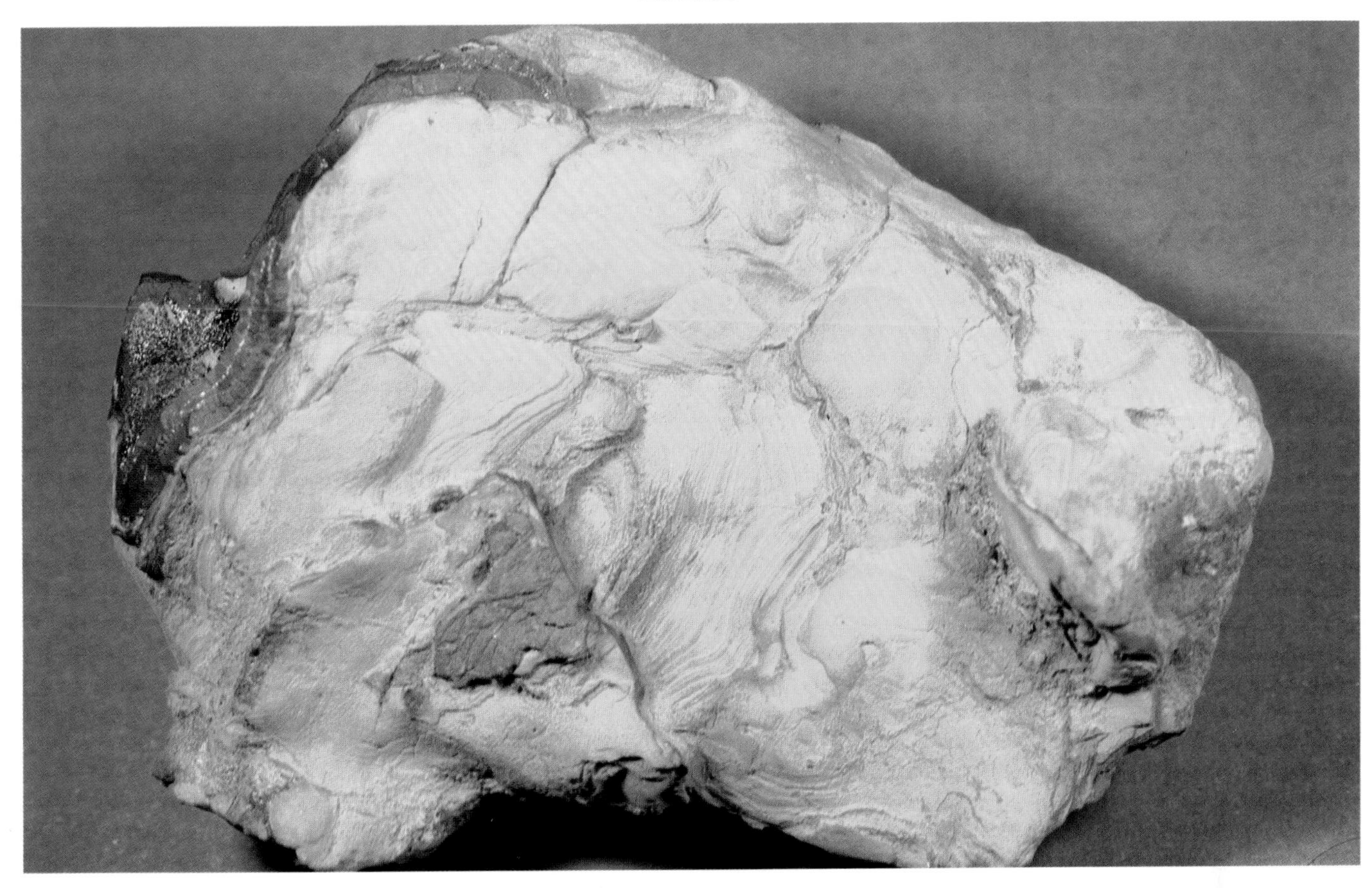

occurring as massive specimens. Limonite is porous and often forms as a crust on rock surfaces as a result of the alteration through weathering of iron-bearing formations. Goethite forms in a similar way through the oxidation of iron deposits.

Above: *Limonite is similar in chemistry to goethite but different in colour (yellowish) and form (massive). This specimen, from Staffordshire, UK, is 10cm (4in) across.*

Brucite [$Mg(OH)_2$]

Brucite occurs as tabular or fibrous crystals in the hexagonal system and as massive specimens. It is a pale-coloured mineral, usually being greenish or white, and has a white streak. It cleaves into thin fibres or flat sheets, and has an uneven fracture. The lustre is a helpful identification feature, being waxy or pearly. Brucite can be scratched easily with a coin, having a hardness of only 2½, and its density is low at 2.4. It has a similar appearance to talc but is harder. Both minerals form in metamorphosed sedimentary rocks. Brucite occurs in marble, often giving the rock an attractive pattern of pale green veins. It can also be found in serpentinite and low-grade schists.

Below: *Brucite, made of magnesium hydroxide, often occurs as delicate greenish veins in metamorphic rocks such as marble. This massive specimen is 6cm (2½in) across.*

QUARTZ

Quartz [SiO_2]

Quartz often occurs as very well-formed hexagonal prismatic crystals, with frequent twinning. Massive specimens are common. Quartz has a vitreous lustre and its colour is so variable that names have been given to many of the colour variants. Colourless quartz is rock crystal, and the common white variety is milky quartz. The semi-precious variety with a purple colour is amethyst, and rose quartz is pink. Cairngorm or smoky quartz varies from brownish to very dark brown. Green quartz is called prase, and the yellow variety is citrine, also used as a gemstone. The streak is always white. One of the characteristic features of quartz is its lack of cleavage; it breaks with an uneven or conchoidal fracture. Quartz is one of the hardest common minerals and defines 7 on the scale. The density is average at 2.65. This is a very common and widely occurring mineral, easily recognized by its lack of cleavage and its hardness. It is an essential component of many igneous rocks and is especially common in granites. Many metamorphic and sedimentary rocks are rich in quartz, and it also frequently occurs as a hydrothermal vein mineral.

Above: *Quartz, formed of silicon dioxide, is one of the hardest common minerals. Fine crystals often occur in rock cavities. Note the hexagonal pyramids capping the prismatic crystals. This specimen is 15cm (6in) across.*

Opal [$SiO_2.nH_2O$]

Opal cannot be classified in a crystal system as it occurs in an amorphous habit, as stalactitic shapes, globular masses and thin veins. This mineral is well known for its shimmering colours, which vary from pink and blue to black. The colours are very subtle and soft, and for this reason it is sought after as a gemstone. Optical refraction within the body of a piece of opal, where the light dances among the tightly packed globules of material, is possibly the reason for its brilliance. The lustre is usually vitreous but may be resinous or even pearly, and opal breaks without cleavage but with a conchoidal fracture. Though of low density at 2.0 to 2.5, opal is quite hard at 5½ to 6½. The hardness and the lack of crystals plus the 'fire' of opal help to distinguish it from quartz. Opal forms at low temperatures as a result of precipitation from solutions rich in silica, usually in veins and hollows in rocks. It can be seen on the front cover (left-hand panel).

Below: *Chalcedony is chemically the same as quartz but forms in the stalactitic and botryoidal habits. Here, finger-like masses have formed in a rock cavity 25cm (10in) across.*

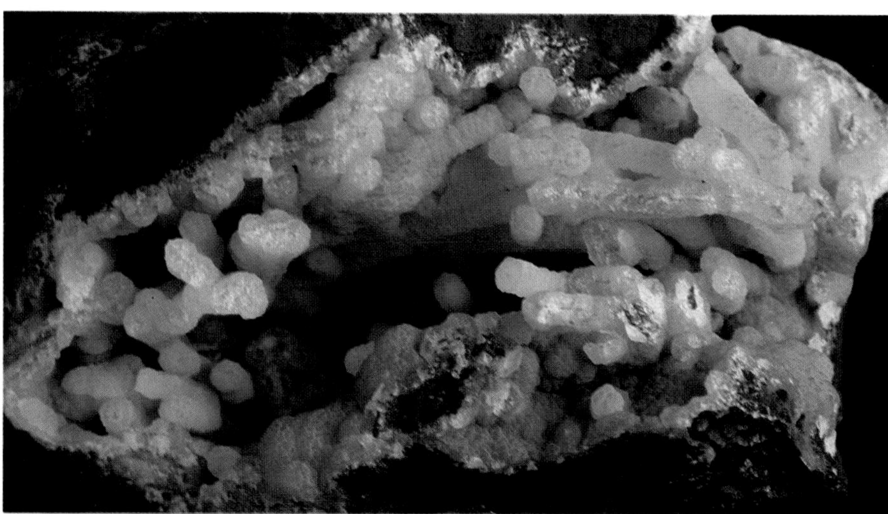

Chalcedony [SiO_2]

Chalcedony is chemically the same as quartz but the structure is different in that chalcedony is made up of micro-crystalline silica with minute crystals interspaced with pores. The hardness is similar to that of quartz at 6½ to 7, and the density is 2.6. It is not easy to assign chalcedony to a crystal system, but hexagonal is usually the one chosen. The lustre is vitreous or waxy, and a great many varieties of chalcedony occur, many typified by both habit and colour. The streak is white. The photograph shows very typical bubbly fingers of chalcedony growing into a rock cavity. Often chalcedony occurs in concentric bands of different colours. It is then called agate and is cut and polished for a variety of semi-precious uses. Crystals of quartz may fill the central part of the cavity in which the bands of agate develop. The formation of these various types of chalcedony is the result of precipitation from solutions running into cavities such as the vesicles in basaltic lavas. These infilled cavities are often called geodes, and when the basalt is weathered the hard quartz-filled geodes remain.

FELDSPARS

Orthoclase [$KAlSi_3O_8$]

Orthoclase forms prismatic and tabular crystals classified in the monoclinic system. The streak is white but the colour is very variable, ranging from white to grey, green and pink. The green variety is called amazonstone, and pink is a common colour in many igneous rocks; for example, many granites owe their reddish colour to the presence of pink crystals of orthoclase. Orthoclase defines hardness 6 on the scale and this property is valuable in its identification. When broken, orthoclase fractures conchoidally or unevenly, and two cleavage directions may be visible. The density is average at 2.6, and there is a pearly or vitreous lustre. Orthoclase has another property which helps to distinguish it from plagioclase. This is its simple twinning. When a specimen, often one in a rock, is examined, it appears as if there is a join through the centre. This is in fact the edge of the plane between two twinned crystals. As the specimen is turned, light falls on each crystal separately. A common variety of orthoclase is microcline, which, when examined under some magnification, is seen to have a 'cross-hatched' structure. This is a result of twinning. As well as being a major constituent of many igneous rocks, orthoclase also occurs in metamorphic gneisses and schists. It may be found in arkoses (sandstones) as grains derived from igneous rocks.

Above: *Orthoclase, a silicate of potassium and aluminium, occurs in many igneous rocks. Each specimen of these two colour variants is 8cm (3¼in) long. Both come from pegmatites.*

Plagioclase [$NaAlSi_3O_8$ to $CaAl_2Si_2O_8$]

Plagioclase varies in its chemistry. This is possible because of the substitution of sodium for calcium in the crystal lattice. Calcium-rich plagioclases tend to be found in igneous rocks which have crystallized at very high temperatures, for example basalts, while the sodium-rich varieties occur in lower-temperature rocks like granites. There is a continuous series of plagioclase feldspars, from calcium-rich anorthite to sodium-rich albite. As a magma freezes, plagioclases can form at every temperature interval because of the substitution of sodium for calcium as the temperature drops. It is often impossible to distinguish the varieties of plagioclase without the help of a powerful microscope and a thin section of the mineral-bearing rock. Some varieties, however, such as labradorite, with its blue play of colours called schillerization, are not difficult to identify.

Plagioclase forms as prismatic crystals in the triclinic system, and can also be tabular or massive in habit. The streak is white, but the colours vary from milky white to green and grey, the blues of labradorite and occasionally pink. There is a vitreous lustre, and when broken the uneven fracture or two cleavage planes can be seen. Plagioclase is slightly harder than orthoclase, being 6½. The density is between 2.6 and 2.75. Plagioclase shows twinning, but of a more complex nature than that of orthoclase. In plagioclase there is repeated twinning which shows itself as many thin bands, especially on cleavage surfaces. When seen in thin section under the microscope, this twinning appears as alternating dark and light stripes. Plagioclase occurs as an essential mineral in many igneous rocks as well as in schists and gneisses and as grains in detrital sediments.

Below: *Plagioclase, an aluminium silicate of sodium or calcium (or both), is common in many igneous rocks. This typical pale-coloured specimen is 10cm (4in) across.*

SILICATES

Tremolite–actinolite [$Ca_2Mg_5Si_8O_{22}(OH)_2$ to $Ca_2(Mg,Fe)_5Si_8O_{22}(OH)_2$]

The minerals in this series of amphiboles form fibrous or radiating crystals which are thin and prismatic in habit. With a white streak, the colour varies from greenish to grey, and the lustre is vitreous. The density varies according to the proportion of iron in the mineral, from 2.9 to 3.4. The hardness varies from 5 to 6. When broken the excellent prismatic cleavage can be seen; the fracture is uneven. Both these minerals are common in metamorphic rocks, tremolite occurring in serpentinites and marbles, while actinolite, as in the sample from north-west Scotland shown here, is encountered in metamorphosed basic igneous rocks.

Hornblende [$(Ca,Na)_{2-3}(Mg,Fe,Al)_5(Si,Al)_8O_{22}(OH)_2$]

This is another common amphibole. It is a very dark green or black vitreous mineral, with a greyish-brown streak, which forms as prismatic monoclinic crystals. It can also have a fibrous habit or occur as granular specimens. The fracture is uneven but an important identification feature is the cleavage, which consists of two planes intersecting at 60° and 120°. Hornblende is hard at 5 to 6 and has a density of 3.4.

Below: *Actinolite, seen here as small greenish crystals set in a matrix of rock from an altered basic igneous intrusion. The specimen, from northern Scotland, is 6cm (2½in) across.*

Augite [$(Ca,Mg,Fe,Ti,Al)(Al,Si)_2O_6$]

Augite is a very common pyroxene. It forms squat crystals of prismatic habit which are classified in the monoclinic system. The cleavage is a characteristic feature and enables augite to be distinguished from the outwardly similar amphibole hornblende. It has two cleavage planes intersecting at 90° (compared with hornblende's 60° and 120°). The fracture is uneven. Augite may also be slightly harder than hornblende at 6½, and its density varies from 3.2 to 3.6. It is a dark green or black mineral with a greyish streak, and it is commonly found in basic igneous rocks, such as basalts and gabbros, and some ultra-basic rocks, for example pyroxenite.

Above: *Tremolite often occurs in thin fibrous bands of prismatic crystals and is common in certain metamorphic rocks. This specimen measures 15cm (6in) across.*

Diopside [$CaMgSi_2O_6$]

Diopside also forms prismatic monoclinic crystals but can occur as fibrous masses. It has the characteristic pyroxene cleavage like

Above: *Olivine, a silicate of iron and magnesium, often occurs in basaltic lavas, as in the case of this rounded mass from the Canary Islands. It is 15cm (6in) across.*

Below: *Dark-coloured almandine garnet set into mica schist – a common occurrence. The biggest of these garnets, from Norway, is 1cm (3/8in) in diameter.*

that of augite and an uneven fracture. With a grey streak, diopside is not as dark-coloured as augite and has a greenish tint. The lustre is vitreous, and the hardness varies from 5 to 6. The density is 3.4. As well as occurring in basic igneous rocks, diopside is also found in marbles derived from the metamorphism of impure limestones.

Olivine [$(Mg,Fe)_2SiO_4$]

Olivine forms a series with varying chemistry. The magnesium-rich end of the series, called forsterite, has the formula Mg_2SiO_4, and the iron-rich type of olivine, fayalite, is Fe_2SiO_4. The variety of forsterite which is used as a gemstone is peridot. Olivine forms crystals in the orthorhombic system, but the habit is usually granular masses rather than crystals. The specimen photographed shows this granular habit. With a vitreous lustre, olivine may have a brownish or yellow colour but is more often a pale green. The streak has no colour. When broken, olivine has virtually no cleavage but a conchoidal fracture. This is a very hard mineral, measuring between 6½ and 7, and its density is variable with fayalite measuring 4.3 and forsterite 3.2. It is a widespread mineral in many igneous rocks, especially those of basic and ultra-basic composition. One ultra-basic rock, dunite, is composed almost entirely of olivine. The basaltic rocks recovered from the moon contain olivine, as do certain meteorites.

Garnet

Garnet has a complex chemistry but is essentially a silicate of metals, such as calcium, magnesium, iron and manganese, with aluminium or chromium. Many varieties have been named; for example, the specimen shown here is almandine, which has the formula $Fe_3Al_2Si_3O_{12}$. Others include the deep red pyrope – $Mg_3Al_2Si_3O_{22}$ – and grossular – $Ca_3Al_2Si_3O_{12}$ –, which can be yellow, green or red. Very good crystals are common in garnets; these are usually complex forms within the cubic system. Garnet may also be massive or granular. This is a mineral with a resinous or vitreous lustre and a grey streak. Because of their rich colours and their hardness of 6½ to 7½, garnets are much used as gemstones. Density is 3.5 to 4.3, depending on precise chemistry, and when broken, garnet shows no cleavage but a subconchoidal fracture. Garnets are common in many rocks, especially metamorphic schists, as illustrated, and in ultra-basic igneous rocks.

Tourmaline $[Na(Mg,Fe,Li,Mn,Al)_3Al_6(BO_3)_3Si_6O_{18}(OH,F)_4]$

Tourmaline is a very complex silicate. It often forms excellent prismatic crystals in the hexagonal system which have longitudinal striations, though it can also be massive in habit. With a vitreous lustre, tourmaline varies in colour from black to dark green and blue. Occasionally crystals change from green to pink along their length. The streak is colourless. When tourmaline is broken, there is a very indistinct cleavage and a conchoidal fracture. It is a hard mineral at 7 and has a density of 2.9 to 3.2. The best crystals of tourmaline are from pegmatite and granite. It also occurs in some metamorphic rocks like schist and gneiss.

Right: *A fine prismatic crystal of tourmaline, and some smaller prisms set in a matrix of pale-coloured quartz. Dark green is just one colour variant. The specimen is from Cornwall, UK, and the large crystal is 6cm (2½in) long.*

Left: *Muscovite, a silicate commonly referred to as white mica, is recognised by its flaky, transparent crystals with a vitreous lustre. Each flake here is 5cm (2in) across.*

Muscovite $[KAl_2(AlSi_3O_{10})(OH,F)_2]$

Muscovite is a type of mica and forms flaky crystals of tabular habit which are classified in the monoclinic system. These crystals are silvery-white in colour, with a white streak and a glittery vitreous lustre. When broken the fracture is very uneven but the cleavage allows the plates of muscovite to be split into many thinner fragments. With a density of 2.8, muscovite is noted for its lack of hardness at 2½. This is a common mineral in igneous rocks, especially granites, and also in metamorphic gneisses and schists. Some sandstones are rich in mica, which lies on the bedding planes.

Biotite $[K(Mg,Fe)_3AlSi_3O_{10}(OH,F)_2]$

Biotite is another variety of mica. It, too, forms flaky tabular crystals, often with a pseudo-hexagonal outline, and varies in colour from black to dark brown. (The closely related mica mineral phlogopite is a yellowish-brown colour and lacks iron in its chemical structure.) The cleavage and fracture are as for muscovite, cleaving into thin flexible flakes with uneven fractured margins. The lustre may be metallic in weathered specimens but is otherwise vitreous. The hardness is from 2 to 3, and the density 2.8 to 3.2. Biotite is also common in many igneous rocks, especially granites, and metamorphic rocks such as gneisses and schists.

Talc [$Mg_3Si_4O_{10}(OH)_2$]

Talc commonly occurs as massive specimens or tabular masses classified in the monoclinic system. As in the specimen shown here, talc can also be botryoidal in habit. The colour is usually greyish or pale green, and the streak is white. This is very easy to obtain because talc is one of the softest of minerals, defining 1 on the hardness scale. The density is 2.8. When broken, talc has an uneven fracture and a basal cleavage. The lustre is dull or pearly, and talc has a greasy feel, sometimes being called soapstone. This fairly common mineral forms when ferromagnesian minerals are altered. It can be found in many metamorphic rocks such as schists and marbles.

Above: *Talc. This is one of the softest minerals. It is a hydrated silicate of magnesium and occurs in schists and marbles. The specimen shown here is from Val Trebbia in Italy and shows a botryoidal habit. It measures 10cm (4in) across.*

Natrolite [$Na_2Al_2Si_3O_{10}.2H_2O$]

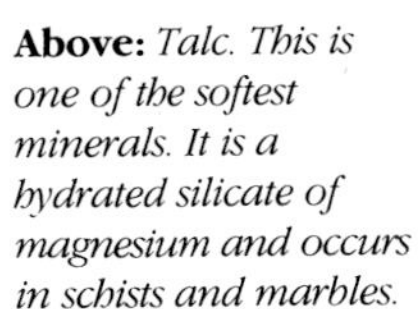

This zeolite forms fine crystals with an acicular (needle-like) habit which often radiate from a centre, as in the photograph. These are classified in the orthorhombic system. With a vitreous lustre, natrolite has a white colour and streak, a prismatic cleavage and an uneven fracture. The hardness is quite high at 5, while at 2.3 the density is below average.

Below: *Natrolite. This zeolite mineral shows a radiating habit with acicular crystals. These often grow in cavities in basaltic lavas. The specimen shown here originated in exactly this way. It comes from Northern Ireland and measures 4cm (1½in) across.*

Beryl [$Be_3Al_2Si_6O_{18}$]

Beryl often forms excellent hexagonal prismatic crystals, frequently of huge size. One such crystal weighed over 25 tonnes and was 9m (30ft) in length. With a vitreous lustre and a white streak, beryl has a variety of colours. It is often pale green or grey; the transparent green form is emerald (this can be seen on the front cover in the bottom right-hand panel), while blue beryl is aquamarine and yellow is heliodor. All are prized as gemstones. When broken, there is a very poor cleavage and a conchoidal fracture. Beryl has a great hardness of 7½ to 8 and a density of 2.6 to 2.9. This mineral occurs in pegmatites and granites. It is sometimes found in alluvial sands originating from primary igneous rocks by erosion.

Kyanite [Al_2SiO_5]

Kyanite forms thin, often bright blue, blade-shaped crystals in the triclinic system. The colour may also be green, grey or white, and the streak is white. With an uneven fracture and a fine two-directional cleavage, kyanite has a hardness of 6 to 7 when scratched across the cleavage surfaces but only 4 to 5 along them. The lustre is often pearly but can be vitreous. Kyanite is found in highly metamorphosed rocks, such as gneisses, where it can be used to estimate the grade of metamorphism.

PHOSPHATES

Apatite [$Ca_5(PO_4)_3(F,Cl,OH)$]

Apatite often forms stubby prismatic crystals which are in the hexagonal system. It also occurs in granular or massive habit. Usually the colour is yellowish-green, though it can be brown, red or grey. The streak is white. Often the lustre is vitreous, but a resinous quality is commonly observed. Apatite is a very brittle mineral with poor cleavage and an uneven or conchoidal fracture. The hardness is the definition of 5 on the hardness scale, and the density not far above average at 3.3. Some forms of apatite give a very strong fluorescence when ultra-violet light is applied to them. This mineral has a varied occurrence. It is found in many igneous rocks, especially lavas, and in some hydrothermal veins. Metamorphosed marbles may contain apatite, as can the fossils of bones.

Pyromorphite [$Pb_5(PO_4)_3Cl$]

Pyromorphite crystallizes in the hexagonal system with crystals which are prismatic. It also forms fibrous and granular aggregates. The streak is cream-coloured but the colour varies from green to yellow and brown. When broken, there is a good prismatic cleavage and an uneven fracture. The lustre is resinous, and the hardness varies from 3½ to 4. The density is high at 6.5. Pyromorphite forms in veins containing lead minerals where weathering and alteration have occurred.

Torbernite [$Cu(UO_2)_2(PO_4)_2.8{-}12H_2O$]

Torbernite is a source of uranium, but not as important a source as autunite. It has tabular crystals which are classified in the tetragonal system, their outline commonly having a square appearance. With a pearly lustre, torbernite is a bright green colour and has a pale green streak. Broken specimens show an uneven fracture and a basal cleavage. This is a very soft mineral with a hardness of only 2½ (the same as a fingernail), and the density is 3.3. Easily recognized by its colour and radioactivity, torbernite occurs in veins of copper and uranium-rich pitchblende (UO_2) which have undergone chemical change.

Right: *As well as occurring as traces on rock surfaces, as here, torbernite can form tabular crystals. This typically bright green sample, from Cornwall, UK, is 10cm (4in) across.*

Wavellite [$Al_3(PO_4)_2(OH)_3.5H_2O$]

Wavellite forms radiating aggregates which have a spherulitic three-dimensional form. This can be clearly seen in the photograph, in which many of the small rounded pieces are broken. This mineral is classified in the orthorhombic system and has a pale green or brownish colour. The streak is white. Though the density is low at 2.4, the hardness is 3½ to 4. The broken mineral has an uneven fracture and a prismatic cleavage. The radiating structure is its best identification feature, and it forms on joint and fracture planes of rocks. This mineral has been exploited for making phosphatic fertilizer.

Autunite [$Ca(UO_2)_2(PO_4)_2.10–12H_2O$]

Autunite is similar to torbernite in many ways and likewise forms square-shaped crystals in the tetragonal system. The habit may be lamellar and tabular. Autunite is often bright yellow in colour, with a yellow streak. The cleavage and fracture are as for torbernite, being basal and uneven respectively. Autunite has a hardness of 2½ and a density of 3.2, with a pearly to vitreous lustre. This radioactive mineral, which forms as a result of the alteration of uranium deposits, was one of the main ores of uranium exploited during the Second World War.

Above: *Wavellite has a spherulitic habit which shows internal radiating structures when broken. It forms in cavities and fracture zones. This specimen, from Devon, UK, is 5cm (2in) across.*

Below: *Autunite, being radioactive, should be housed in a special container with warning signs. Typically bright yellow, it can be greenish. This specimen is 6cm (2½in) across.*

CHROMATES

Crocoite [$PbCrO_4$]

Crocoite forms prismatic crystals in the monoclinic system, which usually occur as acicular bundles; it can also be massive and granular. The colour is very distinctive, being bright orange or red, or sometimes brown, and the streak is yellow. There is a vitreous lustre, and the mineral is brittle, breaking with prismatic cleavage or an uneven fracture. It is easily scratched with a coin, having a hardness of 2½ to 3. Because it contains lead in its chemical structure the density is high at 6.0. Crocoite forms in the parts of lead-bearing veins which have suffered alteration, especially by oxidation.

Below: *Crocoite. This mineral is composed of lead chromium oxide and has a high density. The specimen shown here exhibits the characteristic thin, acicular crystals of orange-red colour. It is from Dundas Mine in Tasmania and is 3cm (1¼in) in diameter.*

MOLYBDATES

Wulfenite [$PbMoO_4$]

Wulfenite occurs as tabular crystals classified in the tetragonal system. It has a characteristic yellowish colour which often has a brownish tint. The streak is white. The lustre varies from adamantine to resinous, and when broken, wulfenite produces a conchoidal fracture and a cleavage which is pyramidal. The hardness is similar to that of crocoite at 3, but the density is higher at 7.0. Another lead mineral, it forms in the altered parts of veins containing minerals of lead and molybdenum.

Below: *Wulfenite. The beautiful yellow, tabular crystals of this oxide of lead and molybdenum are well shown in this specimen from Morocco. It is a mineral of high density and can be found in lead-bearing veins. The specimen is 12cm (4¾in) across.*

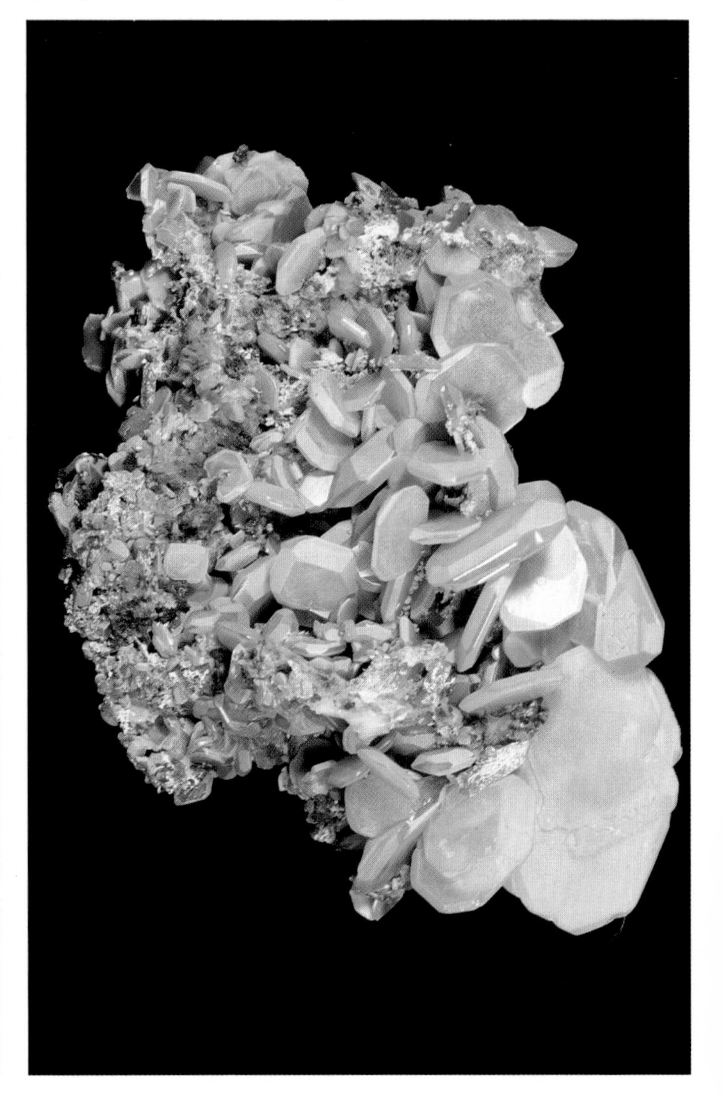

ARSENATES

Mimetite [$Pb_5(AsO_4)_3Cl$]

Mimetite forms prismatic crystals in the hexagonal system. When these crystals are barrel-shaped, the mineral is called campylite, as in the specimen photographed. The colour varies from brown to yellow and greenish-yellow, always with a white streak. The lustre, as with wulfenite, varies from adamantine to resinous, but mimetite is harder at 3½ and slightly denser at 7.2. When broken, there is no cleavage and the fracture is subconchoidal. Mimetite is soluble in a number of acids and gives off a smell similar to that of garlic. This is another mineral of bright colour found in the alteration zones of lead-bearing veins, often in association with arsenopyrite.

Below: *This variety of mimetite, characterised by barrel-shaped crystals, is called campylite. It is composed of lead chloride and arsenic oxide. The specimen is from Cumbria, UK, and is 6cm (2⅜in) across.*

Below: *Vanadinite. The hexagonal prisms characteristic of this red-coloured, high-density mineral are well shown here. The specimen is from the Atlas Mountains in Morocco and measures 4.5cm (1¾in) across.*

VANADATES

Vanadinite [$Pb_5(VO_4)_3Cl$]

Vanadinite forms as characteristic short hexagonal crystals of prismatic habit which are sometimes hollow or rounded. With a whitish-yellow streak, vanadinite has a very rich red colour, though it can also be brown or yellow. It has a pyramidal cleavage and an uneven or conchoidal fracture. The density is high at 7.1, and the hardness is 3. This mineral has some economic use as an ore of vanadium (alloyed with steel and iron for extra strength and wear) and it is found in the alteration zones of lead veins.

Glossary

A

Acid rocks
Igneous rocks which contain more than 10 per cent quartz and more than 65 per cent total silica. This group includes granite and rhyolite.

Agate
A semi-precious form of quartz which has a banded structure, often in concentric rings.

Amphibole
A category of ferro-magnesian silicate minerals, including hornblende. They are important igneous rock formers.

Amygdales
Infilled gas bubble cavities, usually in lavas.

Aureole
The region around an igneous intrusion, or beneath a lava flow, which is so affected by heat that contact metamorphism has occurred there.

B

Basic rocks
Igneous rocks containing less than 10 per cent quartz and between 45 and 55 per cent total silica. Such rocks include gabbro and basalt.

Batholith
A very large igneous intrusion, many miles in diameter, formed at depth in the Earth's crust and often made of granite, though other coarse-grained rocks also occur.

Bedding plane
The surface of deposition in sedimentary rocks. The bed (stratum) exists between bedding planes. These were probably horizontal when originally formed.

Breccia
A coarse-grained sedimentary rock with angular fragments. These particles accumulate through mechanical weathering, as in scree, or along faults.

C

Chert
A form of silica which occurs as discrete masses in limestone. It may have an organic origin. The crystals in chert can only be seen under high magnification.

Cleavage
This term has two uses. In the case of rocks it refers to the thin planes of parting in slates developed during low-grade regional metamorphism by the parallel alignment of flaky mica and clay minerals. In the case of minerals cleavage refers to the way some minerals break along pre-determined planes related to their atomic structure. Cleavage planes are quite flat and reflect the light evenly.

Conchoidal
Describes a curved or shell-shaped fracture produced when some minerals and rocks break.

Concordant
A term used to indicate that an intrusive igneous rock body has formed parallel to existing rock structures such as bedding planes. Sills are concordant minor intrusions.

Country rock
The pre-existing rock which is invaded by an igneous intrusion.

D

Dendritic
Describes a tree-like pattern or structure developed in some minerals. Copper, silver and pyrolusite may have this habit.

Detrital
Describes fragments of rocks and minerals derived by weathering and erosion from pre-formed rock. Detrital fragments form sedimentary rocks, including sandstones.

Diagenesis
The various processes which turn unconsolidated sediment into hard rocks. Both chemical and physical processes are involved and they occur at no great pressure or temperature.

Differentiation
The processes which cause a certain type of magma to form two or more different igneous rocks.

Discordant
When an igneous intrusion cuts across pre-formed rock structures it is said to be discordant. A dyke is a common discordant intrusion.

Dyke
A small-scale, sheet-shaped igneous intrusion which is discordant. Dykes are often vertical, and dolerite is a common dyke-forming rock.

E

Eclogite
A rock of basic or ultra-basic composition made of pyroxene and garnet. It is coarse-grained and of metamorphic origin.

Equigranular
A term applied to the texture of a rock when all the grains or crystals are the same size.

Erosion
The breakdown of rock during, and by, movement.

Euhedral
Describes crystals in a rock which are well-formed; for example, the phenocrysts of feldspar in a porphyritic granite.

Evaporite
A mineral or rock formed when saline water dries up. The minerals halite and gypsum and the rocks dolomite and marl are evaporites.

Extrusive
An igneous rock formed on the surface from the crystallization of lava, i.e. a volcanic rock.

F

Fault
A break in the crustal rocks which has relative displacement on either side.

Ferro-magnesian minerals
Silicate minerals which contain iron and magnesium. This group includes amphiboles, pyroxenes, olivine and biotite.

Foliation
A term generally applied to metamorphic rocks such as schist, in which the parallel orientation of micas produces a wavy texture.

G

Gangue
In a mineral vein there is often a variety of minerals. If the vein is exploited for ores of metals, such as lead or zinc, the other minerals in the vein, e.g. calcite, quartz and baryte, are of no economic significance. These are gangue minerals.

Graphic texture
This is an intergrowth of feldspar and quartz which occurs in some granites. On a smooth rock surface it may appear like hieroglyphic writing.

H

Hopper crystals
Crystals which have hollowed faces. They are common in the cubic crystals of halite.

Hydrothermal fluids
High-temperature waters deep in the crust from which minerals may be precipitated and which may dissolve rocks.

Hypabyssal
Refers to the relatively shallow depth at which some igneous bodies cool. Between volcanic and plutonic.

I

Intermediate rocks
Igneous rocks which chemically are between acid and basic, having a total silica content of between 65 and 55 per cent. Syenite and andesite are in this group.

Igneous rocks
Rocks which have formed as the result of the cooling and freezing of lava or magma.

Intrusive
An igneous rock which has formed in and among other crustal rocks. Its intrusion may be forceful.

L

Laccolith
An igneous rock mass intruded in the form of a flat-based dome.
Lava
Extrusive igneous rock; volcanic rock.
Limestone
A sedimentary rock composed of much calcium carbonate and/or magnesium carbonate along with other material – for example, clay and detrital fragments. The calcareous fraction can be either organic or inorganic.

M

Magma
Molten rock below the surface of the Earth. When erupted it is called lava.
Matrix
The body of a rock, discounting any large crystals or inclusions.
Magmatic segregation
The concentration of certain minerals, often economically valuable metals, in particular regions of a magma body.
Metamorphism
The alteration brought about in crustal rocks by temperature and pressure changes, and the influence of migrating fluids. Melting does not occur but profound changes can nevertheless take place.
Migmatite
A mixed rock containing elements of both acid and basic igneous types, often found in areas of extreme igneous and metamorphic activity.
Mylonite
A rock formed along the plane of a major thrust fault by the pulverization and grinding of the rocks involved. It consists of crushed and streaked-out fine-grained fragments.

O

Orogeny
A period of mountain building. This process may take many tens of millions of years.
Ophitic
The texture of an igneous rock in which lath-shaped feldspar crystals are enclosed in pyroxene.

P

Pegmatite
An exceptionally coarse-grained granitic rock.
Pelitic
Describes mud or clay sediments. Another term is 'argillaceous'.
Pinacoid
With two parallel crystal faces.
Phenocryst
A large euhedral crystal set in the matrix of an igneous rock.
Placers
Certain minerals which, because of high specific gravity or resistance to erosion, accumulate after weathering and erosion in alluvial sands.
Plutonic
Describes the environment of deep igneous activity, as opposed to the hypabyssal and volcanic environments.
Porphyritic
Describes an igneous texture in which large crystals (phenocrysts) are set into a relatively fine matrix.
Porphyroblast
A well-formed crystal set into the matrix of a metamorphic rock, such as pyrite in slate.
Pyroxene
A class of ferro-magnesian silicates, including augite and diopside. They are important in many igneous rocks, especially basalts and gabbros.

R

Recrystallization
Crystals from a rock matrix may pass into solution before developing into a mass of new crystals. This recrystallization can occur during metamorphism.
Reversible dehydration
The two-way process of water being taken into and lost from a mineral's structure.
Rock
In the strict geological sense a rock is any aggregate of mineral particles, either unconsolidated or hard and solid.
Rhombdodecahedron
A crystal form with twelve rhomb-shaped faces.

S

Sediment
The particles derived from pre-formed rocks by weathering and erosion. Volcanic dust and some organic matter can also be included.
Schistosity
When flaky minerals such as micas become aligned during regional metamorphism of medium grade, the wavy planes developed are known as planes of schistosity.
Silicates
The most important group of igneous rock-forming minerals, including pyroxenes, amphiboles and feldspars.
Stock
An intrusive body of igneous rock which is not as big as a batholith and is generally circular in outline.

T

Tectonic
Describes processes associated with movement in the Earth's crust and the resulting structures.
Texture
A term used to describe the shape, size and interrelationship of the grains in a rock.
Thrust
Occurs when a fault with a plane set at a very low angle forces one rock mass over another.
Twinning
Crystals which develop joined together and share a certain crystallographic plane are known as twinned crystals.

U

Ultra-basic rocks
Igneous rocks containing less than 45 per cent total silica. They are very dark in colour and of high density. Their chemistry is similar to that of the upper parts of the Earth's mantle. Many ultra-basic rocks contain very few minerals; dunite, for example, is composed almost entirely of olivine.
Unconformity
An interruption in the sequence of rocks in the Earth's crust. It may be caused by non-deposition or more often by erosion of strata. A time gap thus develops, a certain length of time not being represented by any strata in the region where the unconformity exists.

V

Vesicular
Describes an igneous rock texture with cavities produced by gas bubbles; often found in lavas.
Viscosity
The degree of stickiness of an igneous magma or lava. A lava of low viscosity is runny.

W

Weathering
The breakdown of rocks by *in situ* processes such as chemical and mechanical disintegration.

X

Xenolith
A fragment of country rock caught up in magma or lava and hence often partly altered.

Z

Zeolites
A group of silicate minerals containing water in their chemical structure. They exhibit reversible dehydration.

INDEX

A page reference set in **bold** type refers to the main, headed entry for a rock or mineral; references in *italic* refer to illustration captions.